B. Faujas Saint-Fond

Travels in England, Scotland, and the Hebrides

Undertaken for the purpose of examining the state of the arts, the sciences, natural history and manners, in Great Britain. Vol. 2

B. Faujas Saint-Fond

Travels in England, Scotland, and the Hebrides
Undertaken for the purpose of examining the state of the arts, the sciences, natural history and manners, in Great Britain. Vol. 2

ISBN/EAN: 9783337315597

Printed in Europe, USA, Canada, Australia, Japan

Cover: Foto ©Andreas Hilbeck / pixelio.de

More available books at www.hansebooks.com

TRAVELS

IN

ENGLAND, SCOTLAND,

AND THE

HEBRIDES;

UNDERTAKEN FOR THE PURPOSE OF EXAMINING
THE STATE OF

THE ARTS, THE SCIENCES, NATURAL
HISTORY AND MANNERS,

IN

GREAT BRITAIN:

CONTAINING

Mineralogical Defcriptions of the Country round Newcaftle; or tne Mountains of Derbyfhire; of the Environs of Edinburgh, Glafgow, Perth, and St. Andrews; of Inverary, and other Parts of Argylefhire; and of

THE CAVE OF FINGAL.

IN TWO VOLUMES WITH PLATES.

TRANSLATED FROM THE FRENCH OF

B. FAUJAS SAINT-FOND,

MEMBER OF THE NATIONAL INSTITUTE, AND PROFESSOR
OF GEOLOGY IN THE MUSEUM OF NATURAL
HISTORY AT PARIS.

VOL. II.

LONDON:

PRINTED FOR JAMES RIDGWAY, YORK STREET,
St. JAMES's SQUARE.

1799.

ERRATA.

VOL. II.

Page 10, line 15, for *perspective* read *prospect*.
    29, — 1, for *set* read *sat*.
    39, — 7, for *broke* read *broken*.
    40, for *Mc Quaire*, in the note at the bottom, read *Mc Quaire*.
    47, line 1, for *tetrahedial* read *tetrahedral*.
    47, — 4, dele the comma after truncature.
    47, — 18, for *great* read *greater*.
    51, — 11, for *quartrose* read *quartzose*.
    64, — 6, for *unexpressible* read *inexpressible*.
    81, — 3, after race insert *and*.
    106, — 8, dele *as*.
    117, — 17, dele the comma after susceptible.
    120, — 10, for *ready* read *readily*.
    120, — 12, for *porphyric* read *porphyry*.
    128, — 26, dele the colon after walls.
    128, — 27, for *consist* read *consists*.
    135, — 15, for *these* read *this*.
    140, — 5, after perfect insert *prisms*.
    141, — 2, for *contribute* read *contributed*.
    145, — 2, for *schistus* read *schisti*.
    151, — 23, for *iron* read *inn*.
    154, — 23, for *open* read *opens*.
    164, — 7, for *ingenious* read *injurious*.
    171, — 7, for *schistus* read *schistous*.
    186, — 4, for *where* read *when*.
    191, — 3, dele the comma after crystallization.
    195, — 10, for *opened* read *open*.
    230, — 3, of the note, for *translations* read *transactions*.
    235, — 10, dele *are*.
    272, — 21 for *mephits* read *mephitis*.
    272, — 2 of the note, for *gas* read *gases*.
    278, — 10, for *production* read *productions*.
    303, — 4 of the note, for *Trastlemary* read *Traclestemars*.
    ——— — 9 of the same, after *for* insert *in*.
    313, — 26, dele *to* after *exhibiting*.
    320, — 5, for *seem* read *seemed*.
    324, — 12, for *friendly* read *kindly*.
    338, — 6, for *arrid* read *arid*.
    344, — 20, for *inflammability* read *inflammation*.
    347, — last of the note, after *turn* insert *their attention*.
    348, — 2, for *possess* read *possesses*.

The reader will perceive that the Greek singular *stataclites*, *zeolites*, &c. are in several places used instead of *stalactite*, *zeolite*, &c. These, with other inadvertencies, are left to his own candid correction.

CONTENTS

OF THE

SECOND VOLUME.

CHAPTER I.

DEPARTURE from Oban for the Island of Mull.—Passage of the Sound of Mull.—Small Isle of Niort.—Druidical Monuments.—Arrival at Aros. — — Page 1

CHAPTER II.

Road from Aros to Torloisk.—Stay at Mr. M'Lean's. —Accidents which happened to my Fellow-travellers during their Passage to, and Continuance on, the Isle of Staffa. — — 12

CHAPTER III.

Voyage to Staffa. — — 28

CHAPTER IV.

Description and Natural History of the Isle of Staffa.— General Views. — — 38

CHAP-

CONTENTS.

CHAPTER V.
Stay at Mr. M'Lean's.—Customs and Manners of the Inhabitants of the Isle of Mull. — 63

CHAPTER VI.
Departure from Torloisk.—Stay at Aros.—Visit to two worthy Farmers and Brothers, the Stuarts of Aros.—Excursion to the Mountain of Benmore, the highest in the Isle of Mull.—Stop at Mr. Campbel's, of Knock.—His agricultural Operations.—Curious Lavas.—Departure from Aros for Achnacregs. — 88

CHAPTER VII.
Natural History of the Island of Mull. — 105

CHAPTER VIII.
The Isle of Kerrera. — 144

CHAPTER IX.
Departure from Oban.—Dalmally.—Tindrum.—Lead Ore.—Killin.—River Muscle containing Pearls.—Description of these Pearls and their origin. — 147

CHAPTER X.
Kenmore.—Extraordinary Flux and Reflux of Loch Tay. — 170

CHAPTER XI.
Perth, its Harbour and Manufactures.—Mr. M'Comie, Professor of Mathematics; Mr. M'Greggor, Professor

CONTENTS.

*feſſor of the French Language at the Academy.—
Volcanic Mountain of Kinnoul.—The Agates found
upon it.* — — 181

CHAPTER XII.

*St. Andrews Univerſity.—Library.—Old Churches.—
Natural Hiſtory.* — — 193

CHAPTER XIII.

*Departure from St. Andrews.—Largo.—Leven.—
Dyſart.—Kirkaldy.—Kinghorn.—Leith.—Return
to Edinburgh.* — — 213

CHAPTER XIV.

*Edinburgh.—The Univerſity.—Learned Societies.—
College of Phyſicians.—College of Surgeons.—Cabinet of Natural Hiſtory.—Robertſon.—Smith.—
Black.—Cullen, &c.* — 222

CHAPTER XV.

Departure from Edinburgh.—Itinerary to Mancheſter.—Natural Hiſtory. — 255

CHAPTER XVI.

Mancheſter.—Doctor Henry and his Cabinet.—Cotton Manufactures.—Meſſieurs Thomas and Benjamin Potter.—Charles Taylor. — 260

CHAPTER XVII.

*Departure from Mancheſter.—Buxton; its Mineral
Waters; fine Baths, conſtructed on a Plan by Carr,*
at

viii   CONTENTS.

at the Expence of the Duke of Devonshire, the Proprietor of the Waters.—Doctor Pearson.— Manufacture of Vases and other Articles in Fluor Spar of different Colours.—Cave of Poole's Hole.— Toad-stone, composed of a Basis of Trapp, interspersed with Particles of calcareous Spar, and cracked into prismatic Sections like those of basaltes, though not produced by Fire as the latter has been.   264

CHAPTER XVIII.

Castleton.—Description of the Cave called The Devil's Arse.—Mines of Lead and Calamine, Veins of Fluor Spar.—Lead found in Channel or Catdirt.   —   —   309

CHAPTER XIX.

Derby.—Richard Brown, a Dealer in Curiosities of Natural History.—A Manufacture of Vases, and other Workmanship, in Fluor Spar.   334

CHAPTER XX.

Departure from Derby.—Arrival at Birmingham.— Its numerous Manufactures.—Doctor Withering.— Benjamin Watt.—Doctor Priestly—His House, Library, and his chemical Elaboratory.   338

CHAPTER XXI.

Departure from Birmingham.—Coventry.—Warwick. —Oxford.—Saint Albans.—Barnet.—London.— Return to France.   —   —   349

TRAVELS

TRAVELS

THROUGH

ENGLAND AND SCOTLAND

TO THE

HEBRIDES.

CHAPTER I.

Departure from Oban for the ifland of Mull.—Paſſage of the Sound of Mull.—Small iſle of Niort.— Druidical Monuments.—Arrival at Aros.

I HAD finiſhed my folitary excurſions in the environs of Oban, and was nearly done with arranging my obſervations when the people of the inn announced the arrival of a traveller, who, aſtoniſhed to learn, that there was a Frenchman alone in fo defart a place, begged permiſſion to fee me.

He was a young Britiſh Officer of the name of M'Donald, who had come to wait at Oban for a favourable opportunity of going to the ifle of Sky, which was the place of his nativity.

He had profecuted his earlier ftudies at the Scotch college in Paris; he fpoke the French language tolerably, and was not deficient in information. His arrival was a happy and agreeable rencounter for me. I mentioned to him the object of my journey, and my fpeedy departure for the ifle of Mull, where my fellow-travellers were waiting for me to accompany them to the celebrated cave of Fingal, in the ifle of Staffa.

Mr. M'Donald replied, that though his native country was at no great diftance from that ifland, and though he had often heard of the cave of the father of Offian, his education in France and his travels had not yet given him an opportunity of vifiting a place fo remarkable: but, that if I were kind enough to permit him, he would gladly embrace the occafion of accompanying me thither; and that he would alfo have the pleafure of being ufeful to me in the country, as he underftood the Earfe or Celtic language, the only one ufed in the ifles of the Hebrides.

I accepted the obliging offers of Mr. M'Donald with fo much greater pleafure and gratitude,

gratitude, as they appeared to proceed from a man of a fociable difpofition, and were delivered in a tone of franknefs and affability which prepoffeffed me in his favour: I reflected alfo that it was in his power to do me fome fervices in the ifle of Mull, where he had feveral acquaintance, particularly Mr. M'Lean, to whom the Duke of Argyle had given me letters of recommendation. We now waited only for the arrival of the boat which was to carry us; and which at length entered the harbour in the night of the 23d of September.

The crew confifted of no more than two fifhers from the ifle of Sky, who were clothed in the fafhion of the Hebrides, that is, in the drefs of the Scotch Highlanders. Our veffel had neither decks nor rigging; fhe was of the worft conftruction; and dragged at her ftern a fmall fkiff capable of holding at moft only four perfons.

The fare was agreed upon, and it was fettled that we fhould fet out on the following day; but from fome capricious motive, our boatmen changed their refolution, and wifhed to remain for three days longer. It was not without much flattery, repeated remonftances, and

and a prefent of two bottles of rum, that Mr. M'Donald at laft prevailed on them to make ready for our departure on the next morning.

We left the fhore of Oban, at feven in the morning of the twenty-fourth. The fea, though not tempeftuous, was fomewhat agitated; the winds were variable, and the currents of the entrance of the found of Mull running in oppofition to the tide, obliged our intrepid fifhers to make feveral manœuvres, which were exceedingly laborious, as there were only two of them, and they were deftitute of many articles of tackling. All this, however, was mere fport to men inured to the moft lengthened fatigue, and accuftomed, in the time of the herring-fifhery, to brave all the dangers of this frightful fea.

On clearing the harbour, we came in fight of that fucceffion of iflands which fkirt the found, and exhibit a diverfified picture. The ifle of *Lifemore* was at a very fmall diftance on our right; that of *Kerera* in the oppofite quarter; and the Peaks, or as they are called, *Paps of Jura*, towered above the numerous mountains of the Hebrides. Loch-aber, which the largeft veffels may navigate as high

as

as Fort William, was left behind us. The isle of Mull appeared in view; that of Sky was in the distance; and the continued ridge of Morven, so much celebrated in the songs of Ossian, and which exhibits so various and picturesque an appearance, bordered the right bank of the channel which we sailed along.

In passing near the extremity of the isle of Lismore, I observed, with the aid of my perspective, on a small neighbouring island, which was inhabited, one of those monuments of rude stone known by the Hebridian appellation of *Cairn*.

This monument, of great antiquity, and erected in so desart a situation, naturally attracted my attention. I requested my companion to induce our boatmen to convey us thither; but as this small island, or rather large rock, was surrounded with breakers, they replied, that it would be impossible to approach but in the skiff, and that even in it we should run a considerable risk.

I did not understand a word of the language of our conductors, but I observed one of our seamen preparing to enter the skiff; I confidently followed him, and Mr. M'Donald did the same. The skiff was so small and so very

very shallow, that there was hardly room to seat ourselves in it. The boatman took hold of the oars; Mr. M'Donald sat at the helm, which consisted of the half of an oar, and we pushed off.

Our curiosity in this instance prevailed over our prudence; we were borne along by the current with the rapidity of an arrow, towards the small island, which is called Niort; and it required all the addrefs of our boatman, to land us safely. The isle is about half a mile in circumference, and rises only about twenty-five feet at most above the water. It may be regarded as a great rock, of which the summit is flattened into a small plain. The fury of the waves of this tempestuous sea has laid the rock almost entirely bare, and carried away the small quantity of earth which is formed there by time, so that nothing grows upon it except a few *lichens* and some scurvy grass in the sheltered cavities. The rock is composed of limestone, intermixed with a little clay; it is of a blackish grey colour, and only forms a single mass, in which there is no trace either of beds or banks.

Our

Our attention was much attracted by the kind of rustic pillar which stood on this crag. It was nine feet high, three feet broad, and two feet of average thickness. It is formed of grey granite, in which quartz and mica are predominant. The felt-spar is rather disposed in small streaks than in crystals, and though the texture of the stone is somewhat fissile, it is hard and solid in its fracture.

Though this column possesses some regularity in its form, it does not bear the slightest trace of workmanship. It may be considered as a natural block of a longitudinal shape, taken from the quarry in its rude state, and erected on the highest point of this small isle. It is two feet in the earth, and kept upright by two solid but rustic studs, which give it a very stable foundation*.

* In some quarries of granite, and even at times in porphyric rocks, are found similar blocks divided into parallelopipeds of various degrees of regularity and length. They are the effect merely of the contraction of the matter during the time of the aggregation of the particles. Near the small town of Saint Siphorien-de-Lay, within three leagues of Roane, is a porphyric rock divided into large prisms, of which several are as remarkable for regularity as those of the largest and most perfect columns of basaltes.

Our boatman told Mr. M'Donald that he had often feen this ftone; that it had been placed there by the hands of Offian; and that in feveral other ifles we fhould fee much larger ftones, which had been fet up by the fame perfon. For in the mountains of Scotland, and the Hebrides, every thing that appears great, extraordinary, and wonderful, is uniformly regarded as the work of Offian.

Whatever may be the prevailing traditions refpecting thefe ancient columns, this one evidently difcovers an intention of erecting a fimple but durable monument.

This intention is plainly marked by the kind of ftone which has been felected for the purpofe. One fhould think that it would have been more convenient to employ that of which the iflet itfelf is compofed. But whatever muft have been the motives, whether it was known that the latter was lefs durable than the granite; or whether, from the ufe of iron being unknown by thofe who erected it, it was impoffible for them to cut out a fimple pillar from a calcareous rock which is not feparated in banks; it is neverthelefs true that this ruftic column of granite has been tranfported thither; an undertaking

dertaking which muſt have been attended with great difficulty to men ignorant of the mechanic arts.

Though we ſpent but a very ſhort time in examining this ſtone, it was not without great difficulty that we got back to the veſſel which the currents drove to a conſiderable diſtance, notwithſtanding the efforts that were made to keep near us. We were nearly an hour in regaining her.

We continued our courſe through the ſound of Mull, with the granitic mountains of Morven ſtill on our right. We paſſed very near the old caſtle of *Ardtorniſh*, built upon a point which commands a view of the whole ſound. On our left were the black volcanic rocks of the iſle of Mull. At length, after a navigation of ſeven hours and a half, we entered the bay of Aros in that iſland, where we diſembarked.

I hardly know by what term to denominate, five or ſix houſes in a groupe, and ſeven or eight others ſcattered around, the whole of which taken together, are here called Aros. They can ſcarcely be called a town or a village; they may more properly be termed a hamlet; but by whatever name one may choofe choose to distinguish them, they are certainly inhabited by very kind and hospitable people.

The bay of Aros was anciently defended by a strong castle, which formed the residence of M'Donald of the isles; the ruins of this fortress are still extant; and it appears to have been partly built of basaltic prisms.

We were received with the most frank and hearty welcome by an aged gentleman, who is styled Campbell of Aros. He lives in philosophic contentment in the modest habitation of his fathers; which is a gothic building, standing on a black volcanic rock, totally destitute of verdure, beat by the tempests, and yielding no other perspective than that of a raging sea abounding in shipwrecks.

Mr. Campbell, wrapped in the Hebridian fashion, in a large mantle of variegated stuff, introduced us into his house, and refreshed us with some port wine, sea biscuit, and preserve of myrtil berries. His wife, who was not much younger than himself, seemed much astonished at seeing strangers quit their native country, to visit a region so wild, and so difficult of access. Both of them pressed us very much to remain a few days with them; but as I was anxious to rejoin my
fellow-

fellow-travellers, who were waiting for me at Mr. M'Lean's, of Torloisk, we begged the favour of Mr. Campbell to procure us horses; which he had the goodness immediately to provide. The horses were quite small, and had only a piece of rope for a bridle; but they were pretty strong and inured to the rugged roads of the country. We took leave of the old gentleman and his lady, and pursued our journey.

CHAP-

CHAPTER II.

Road from Aros to Torloisk.—Stay at Mr. M˚Lean's. —Accidents which happened to my fellow-travellers during their paſſage to, and continuance on, the Iſle of Staffa.

THE miles of Scotland, particularly thoſe of the iſles, are nearly double the length of the Engliſh miles. From our ignorance of this difference, we found that we had been much deceived when we were told, that from Aros to Torloisk was only eight miles. Imagining the computation to be by Engliſh miles, as we had ſet off at four in the evening, we conceived that we could eaſily ride that diſtance before dark.

I ought not to forget to mention that Mr. M'Donald, who accompanied me from Oban with the intention of viſiting the iſle of Staffa, had no ſooner reached Aros than he changed his dreſs. He had travelled before in Engliſh regimentals, but upon arriving here he opened his portmanteau, and to my great ſurpriſe, in about half an hour after, appeared in the complete

veſture

vefture of the inhabitants of the ifles : plaid, jacket, kilt, feathered bonnet, buskin-hofe, durk, no part of it was omitted. I was fcarcely able to know him again in this drefs. He told me, that it was the garb of his fathers, that he never appeared in any other when in thefe iflands, and that the wearing of it was a mark of attachment to his fellow-countrymen, with which they were much pleafed.

We fet out on our two little horfes, with two perfons to conduct us and bring them back, ignorant that our way lay acrofs ravines, heaths, marfhes and mountains, difficult of accefs, and without any trace of a road.

Whilft day-light remained, we made pretty good progrefs ; our guides pufhed forward with fuch fpeed, that they often outran our horfes, though they went at a good pace. Thefe two Hebridians were young and handfome; neither ftreams, pools, bogs, nor mountains, could interrupt their courfe ; and I admired their courage, gaiety, and elegant appearance. A blue military bonnet, with a border of red, green, and white, and furmounted with one feather, decorated their heads. A party coloured mantle or plaid hung from the

the right shoulder, and paſſed gracefully over the left arm. They had a waiſt-coat and jacket of the ſame ſtuff. Their thighs and legs were half naked. A Tartan buskin with a ſtout kind of ſhoes, covered the lower part of the latter; and compleated their Roman habit. The poniards in their girdles gave them a military air, and the ſticks in their hands, ſerved to help them over the waters.

Their willingneſs to be uſeful to us rendered them doubly intereſting. They always went before to point out the way to us, returning however at intervals to careſs and animate our horſes, and to enquire whether we had occaſion for their ſervices.

They ſeemed proud and overjoyed at ſeeing a man of diſtinction in the ſame dreſs as themſelves; and teſtified their ſatisfaction by approaching Mr. M'Donald, and telling him, with a ſmile on their faces, in their expreſſive language, that they would follow him to the world's end *.

Night

---

* Johnſon alſo, in his journey to the Weſtern Iſlands of Scotland, praiſes two Highlanders whom he had hired as guides on his way from Inverneſs.

" At

Night now came on, we were yet scarcely half way to the place of our destination. Our guides and our horses soon slackened their pace; the road grew detestable, and we were often obliged to alight, sometimes on the verge of marshes, and sometimes in the midst of heaths, through which we groped our way with extreme difficulty. At length we completely lost our direction. The night was so dark that our horses fell repeatedly, and our guides were greatly perplexed. After thus wandering for a long time without any certain course, we at last descried a light on an elevated situation, to which we directed our steps. We found it to be the castle of Torloisk, where we arrived at eleven, worn out with fatigue, anxiety, and vexation.

We soon discovered, as we entered, that we had now reached our place of destination.

" At Inverness," says he, " we procured three horses
" for ourselves and a servant, and one more for our bag-
" gage, which was no very heavy load.—We took two
" Highlanders to run beside us, partly to shew us the
" way, and partly to take back from the sea-side the
" horses, of which they were the owners. One of them
" was a man of great liveliness and activity, of whom his
" companion said, that he would tire any horse in Inver-
" ness. Both of them were civil and ready-handed. Ci-
" vility seems part of the national character of High-
" landers."

A do-

A domeftic told our guides, that Mr. M'Lean had not yet gone to bed, and that I had been impatiently expected for feveral days.

We were fhewn into a parlour, where I found Mr. M'Lean, to whom I gave the letter which I had from the Duke of Argyle. He received me with the moft obliging kindnefs, and prefented me to his wife, daughter, and feveral other ladies and gentlemen, who were occupied in making a little mufical concert.

Mifs M'Lean, a girl of a moft charming figure, was feated at a harpfichord, on which fhe executed fome excellent Italian mufic. Mr. M'Donald had no need of being introduced, his name was already known, and his drefs fufficiently announced him. We were inftantly overwhelmed with civilities, kindneffes, and delicate attentions, which diffipated all our troubles. Every one around us was fo obliging and fo affable, that from that moment we regarded ourfelves as members of the family.

How powerfully attractive is this rural politenefs, feafoned with expreffions and geftures which announce the moft delicate feeling. We were now on the true foil of

hofpi-

hofpitality; all the inhabitants of the ifland, though it contains a population of fix thoufand fouls, have the fame family-name of M'Lean; they are diftinguifhed by their Chriftian names only, or by that of their refidence; they are almoft all fhepherds or fifhers.

We were informed that my fellow-travellers had failed at five in the morning of the fame day, to vifit the ifle of Staffa; that they would have waited with pleafure to make the voyage in company with me; but the feafon was already fo far advanced, and particularly the fea was fo boifterous in this region, that they had determined to take advantage of an interval of calm, which did not promife a long continuance; fuch was their eager impatience to fee that famous ifle.

They had embarked with a friend of Mr. M'Lean, and their own fervants, in two fmall boats. But they had fcarcely gone four or five leagues, before the weather fuddenly changed, and the fea became tempeftuous. Mr. M'Lean thought it fo rough, that he was afraid they had not been able to effect a landing on the ifle of Staffa, on account of the breakers which furround it, and that they had

had been obliged to take refuge in the ifle of *Iona* or *Ykolmkill*, which is fifteen miles from Staffa, and has a fmall creek.

We expected that the fea would be a little calmer by the next day. We repaired therefore, at an early hour, along with Mr. M'Lean and his family, to the water fide, which was about a furlong from the caftle, to fee whether the boatmen would venture to come for a fupply of provifions; but the fea was ftill more dreadful, and totally impaffable.

We now began to be very uneafy on their account. They were eight in number, including the domeftics, and they had only one day's provifion with them.

The evening arrived without any appearance of them; our anxiety was redoubled, and we paffed a very unhappy night.

On the next day, which was Sunday, and the third day from their departure, I rofe at four in the morning to examine the weather. I difcovered with pleafure that the wind had fomewhat fallen, and that the fea was not fo high. We went, before noon, to take a walk on the bank; and at length, with the aid of a good glafs, we defcried them at a diftance.

They

They arrived at one o'clock, to their own and our great fatisfaction. They were fo emaciated with fatigue, vexation and hunger, were fo much in want of food and reft, and fo uneafy, that they entreated us not to difturb them with any queftions until they were a little refrefhed, and particularly relieved from a multitude of lice that tormented them moft cruelly. " Fly! fly from our ap-
" proach," faid they, " we have brought fome
" good fpecimens of mineralogy, but our col-
" lection of infects is numerous and horrible."
We could not keep from laughing at this ad-
drefs, their gait, and the reftlefs motion of every part of their body. They were in-
ftantly conducted to their apartments, where their firft care was to clean themfelves, and, after eating fomething, to take a few hours repofe.

In the evening they returned to the par-
lour, where they were received with every demonftration of kindnefs. Their appear-
ance was now frefh and elegant; but we, notwithftanding, jocularly asked, whether it was yet fafe to approach them. " We
" have caft off every thing," replied they,
" and of all our evils there remains only the
" itch,

"itch, refpecting which, we can fay nothing,
as it has not yet made itfelf felt."

They then recounted the circumftances of
their unfortunate paffage. Notwithftanding
the fine appearance of the weather on the day
of their departure, fcarcely had they proceeded fix miles, when there arofe a violent
gale, which worked the fea into the moft
terrible commotion. They would have willingly put back, had not the rocks which
fkirt the coaft of Torloisk, rendered it equally
dangerous to approach it at that moment;
the currents and the tide were alfo unfavour-
able to their return. They were, therefore,
obliged to keep the offing, and to brave the
impetuofity of the billows, driven fometimes
in one, and fometimes in another direction,
and every inftant in danger of being fwal-
lowed up, were it not for the addrefs and experience of the boatmen who had been accuftomed to thefe terrible feas from their infancy.

Having, at length, after many ftruggles
and dangers, reached the ifle of Staffa, they
found it ftill more difficult to effect a landing.
By the affiftance however of the people of
the ifle, who, on feeing their diftrefs, threw

out

out fome ropes to them, and by watching a favourable wave, they reached the fhore without any other accident than that of wetting themfelves to the skin.

The coaft however was too rugged and fteep to admit of hauling up the two boats, which were obliged to put off again, and to take fhelter in the ifle of Iona or Ykolmkill, about fifteen miles from Staffa.

Our friends, continuing their recital, informed us, that the only two families who inhabited this fmall ifland, received them with the moft affecting hofpitality, and that the one which was in the moft eafy circumftances invited them to enter their hut, where they were ufhered into the midft of fix children, a woman, a cow, a hog, a dog, and fome fowls.

There was laid out for them a remnant of oaten ftraw which had been ufed to litter the cow for feveral days before. This ferved as their feat, table, and bed. A fire of bad turf, or rather ill-dried fod, lighted in the middle of this cabin, blinded them with fmoak, at the fame time that it dried their clothes and ferved to roaft, in an indifferent manner, fome potatoes, which, with fome milk, were

the

the only articles the place afforded, and thofe in very fmall quantities. The provifions which they had brought with them were confumed at one repaft.

The fea broke upon the ifland with fuch impetuofity, and rufhed into the caves which penetrate its interior with fo much noife, that the hut fhook to its foundation, and our adventurers could get no fleep.

On the next day it rained inceffantly until noon. The fea, far from falling, raged with ftill greater fury; fo that the boatmen could not venture to carry any fupply from the ifle of Iona.

In the afternoon, the rain having ceafed, the captives furveyed the ifland and vifited the cave of Fingal. William Thornton took fome views of it with great care; and they made a collection of the moft curious ftones, among which were fome fine zeolites.

In the evening they had the fame reception, the fame fupper, and the fame bed. A new incident, however, occurred : The mafter of the cottage, his wife, and children lived in fuch a horrid ftate of filth that the place completely fwarmed with vermin. Detachments of lice approached on all fides to pay

pay their refpects to the new lodgers, who were foon entirely covered over with them. Thefe were their moft cruel torment, and formed the object of an occupation which did not allow them a moment's refpite.

On the third day, the fea was fomewhat calmer. Their diftrefs was extreme. They walked repeatedly round the ifland, and afcended the higheft part of it to look for the approach of the boats, which at length made their appearance, and came to deliver our poor friends from their afflicting captivity. After thanking their hofts for their kind offices and hofpitable attention, they took leave of them on their return to Torloifk; where we had the happinefs to welcome them with all the ardour of friendfhip. We congratulated them on their being fo fortunate as to efcape with fuffering only a few days abftinence. Finding them all fafe, it was not without a hearty laugh, that we heard them relate their misfortunes, and particularly the diverting epifode of the lice.

Their account brought to my remembrance, at the moment, a fimilar adventure which happened

happened in the fame ifle, and probably in the fame houfe, to Sir Jofeph Banks, who. fet out from London in the year 1772, on a voyage to Iceland, in company with Solander, James Lind, Gore, Walden, and Troil; and, in paffing, paid a vifit to the fine cave of Fingal, of which he was the firft who gave a defcription.

On their arrival at Staffa, they erected a tent, to pafs the night under it; but the only inhabitant then on the ifland preffed Sir Jofeph fo ftrongly to go to fleep in his hut, that he complaifantly confented, and left the tent to his companions.

On leaving the hut next morning, he difcovered that he was completely covered with lice. He mentioned the circumftance to his hoft in terms of mild reproach. But the latter, who was touched to the quick, perked himfelf up, and affuming a tone of confequence, retorted the accufation in a haughty and fomewhat harfh manner on Sir Jofeph, afferting, that it was he who had imported the lice into his ifland, and obferving, that he might as well have left them behind him in England.

The

The detail of the adventures of my poor friends, did not much encourage me to attempt the fame voyage. Mr. M'Lean alfo did not ceafe to imprefs me with the inconftancy of the weather, the dangers of difembarking on the ifland, the advanced period of the feafon, and his apprehenfions left, could we even feize a favourable moment to waft us thither, we fhould not find it equally eafy to return, and left we fhould be obliged to remain there, not only feveral days like our friends, but perhaps for feveral months.

" I am advanced in years," faid Mr. M'Lean; " I have made feveral voyages
" to India, and I am accuftomed to the fea;
" but I have never yet, from complaifance to
" any of the perfons recommended to my at-
" tention, accompanied them to the ifle of
" Staffa, without having occafion to repent
" the attempt. During the courfe of my
" life I have made this voyage fix times, on
" the moft favourable days and with skilful
" feamen, and every time I met with fome
" dangers, either in going or returning.
" Its coaft is fo rocky, and the fea, which furrounds it, rages in general with fo much
" fury, that the landing, even with the fmall-
" eft

"eft boats, is the moſt terrible of all dan-
"gers*."

All theſe accounts were not very encouraging, eſpecially to one, who, like me, is almoſt always ſick on the water; but curioſity overcame the ſuggeſtions of fear and prudence. What, ſaid I, inceſſantly to myſelf, ſhall I have come in a manner to the very entrance of this renowned cave, and from ſuch a diſtance too, without enjoying a view of it? Shall I thus eaſily forego the opportunity of obtaining new information and inſtructive facts, on a ſubject of natural hiſtory in which I feel ſo much intereſt as that of ancient volcanos? and ſhall I not be able to accompliſh what my fellow-travellers have performed? Or, ſhall I heſitate to encounter the ſame danger? All theſe reflexions irrevocably fixed my determination; and I reſolved to ſet out at ſunriſe next morning, if the ſea ſhould be anywiſe paſſable.

I inſtantly engaged a boat for the purpoſe. Mr. M'Donald ſaid, that he ſhould accompany me, and my intrepid friend, William Thornton, ſcarcely yet recovered from his fatigue,

* "Here," ſays Mr. Pennant, " Æolus may be ſaid to "make his reſidence, and be ever employed in fabricating "blaſts, ſqualls, and hurricanes."

not-

notwithſtanding all the dangers he had already met with, told me, that he was alſo ready to recommence the voyage. This young American had ſo ſtrong a deſire of information, particularly in every thing connected with Natural Hiſtory, that nothing was capable of damping his ardour.

CHAPTER III.

Voyage to Staffa.

NEXT morning at four o'clock, one of our boatmen came to inform us that the weather began to be more moderate, and that it was probable we fhould have a fine day. Having made 'the requifite arrangements on the preceding evening, we were foon ready, and reached the beach before fun-rife.

Our rowers were four young and bold Hebridians, who appeared to undertake this fhort voyage with pleafure; for they are fond of every thing which reminds them of Offian, and they feemed to regard it as a happinefs and honour to conduct ftrangers to the cave of Fingal. We befides, allotted them a quantity of refrefhments, of which, to be prepared againft whatever might happen, we laid in an abundant provifion.

The boat was fo fmall as to be incapable of carrying a fail. Our four feamen feated themfelves on their benches; Mr. M'Donald took hold of the helm, William Thornton and

and myself, set down on a bundle of sea-weed, and we proceeded under the auspices of the genius who presides over the science of Nature, and to whom we addressed a short invocation.

In little more than an hour and an half we doubled the point of the isle of Ulva, opposite to that of Mull, near Torloisk, which we had set out from, and entered on the open sea: we soon found, that in these regions, the ancient and majestic ocean does not require the influence of the northern blast to swell its surface into immense waves.

Continuing our course, we had a view of the volcanic isles of Bacabeg, and the Dutchman's Cap, with those of Lunga, Sky, Gometra, Iona, &c.

We could not have wished for a more agreeable passage at so advanced a season. Our seamen, making Mr. M'Donald their interpreter, assured us, that so fine a day was very uncommon in that country, and seldom occurred twice in the same year. To testify the chearfulness with which it inspired them, they began to chaunt in chorus the songs of Ossian. There is not a native of these islands, from the oldest to the youngest, that is not
able

able to repeat, from memory, long paffages or hymns of that ancient and celebrated bard.

The fongs continued a long time. They confifted of monotonous recitatives, ending in choruffes equally monotonous. Their predominant character was a fort of dignity intermixed with plaintive and melancholy tones. The oars, which always moved in cadence, tended to make the monotony more complete. I became drowfy, and foon fell into a profound fleep.

I know not how long I remained in this ftate; but I was awaked from it by the motion and noife of the feamen, and I was told that we were now clofe upon the ifle of Staffa, and near fome reefs, which required new manœuvres. Here I had an opportunity of witneffing, not without dread, the addrefs and intrepidity of our conductors, who knew how to feize the favourable inftant to avoid being dafhed to pieces, and to choofe the propitious furges which afford a fafe paffage over thofe rocks that render it fo dangerous to approach the ifland.

Two of the inhabitants of the ifland foon made their appearance, and threw down to us us from its craggy height some ropes, with the aid of which and a fortunate wave, we difembarked amidft a cloud of foam.

Thefe two men conducted ourfelves, and our fmall crew, to a level fpot on the higheft part of the ifle, where there ftood two houfes, or rather huts, conftructed of large blocks of lavas and mutilated prifms of bafaltes, they were covered over with green fods, and had no other paffage for the light than the door, which was only three feet high, and the chimney, which confifted of a pyramidal tunnel in the middle of the hut.

The women and children of the two families inftantly came out to meet us, and requefted that we would enter their habitations: but being already informed of their exceffive flovenlinefs, we were inflexible to their entreaties; and juftly preferred to receive their civilities and their compliments in the open air.

Finding, that it was impoffible to prevail with us by the moft obliging geftures, they refolved to fhew the marks of their refpect for us on the fmall efplanade in front of their dwellings.

The

The men, women, and children, first formed themselves in a large circle around us and our seamen. Then one of the women, whose appearance was rendered most disgusting by filth and uglinefs, brought out a large wooden bowl filled with milk, with which she placed herself in the center of the circle. She viewed us all round with attention, and immediately came up to me, and pronouncing some words, presented the bowl with a sort of courtesy. I held out my hands to receive it; but she drank some of it, before she gave it to me. I followed her example, and passed the vessel to William Thornton, who was next to me; he gave it to Mr. M'Donald; and it thus passed from hand to hand, or, more properly, from mouth to mouth, till every person had tasted of it. Having made our acknowledgments for this kindness, they immediately appointed two guides to accompany us to the cave of Fingal, and all the remarkable places of this small isle. We ate a morsel of bread, to take off the edge of our appetite during the walk; as it was agreed upon, that in order to loose as little as possible of so favourable a day, we should postpone taking our repast till we were seated in the boat on our

way

way back. This allowed us fufficient time to fee all the curious objects of the ifland at our eafe, and particularly to direct our attention to that remarkable cave which we had come fo far to view, and which we felicitated ourfelves on being enabled to examine on one of the fineft days of the year.

We went to work, therefore, without lofing a moment of time. I foon arrived at the entrance of this wonderful grotto, which an ancient, but fabulous tradition, regards as the palace of the father of Offian. I was obliged to put off my fhoes in order to avoid flipping into the fea, which rufhed in with great noife. There is no other means of going into the cave, but by proceeding with the utmoft precaution along a fort of cornice on the right fide, about fifteen feet above the furface of the water, and formed of a number of erect bafaltic columns, on the broken tops of which one muft ftep with confiderable dexterity, at the risk of falling into the fea, which extends to the inmoft extremity.

Attention is fo much the more neceffary here, as the ledge upon which the adventurer treads is entirely perpendicular, in fome places not above two feet wide at moft, and confifts folely of unequal prifms, very flippery, and conftantly wet with the foam of the waves and the exudations from above. The light, which comes from the grand entrance only, diminifhes gradually as he proceeds inwards, and thus encreafes the difficulty of his path.

I ceafed not to view, to review, and to meditate upon this fuperb monument of nature, the form of which bears fo ftrong a refemblance to the work of art, though the latter can certainly claim no fhare in it. I took all the dimenfions of it, with the affiftance of Mr. M'Donald, whofe fervices were of the greateft ufe to me. I wifhed to obferve the moft fcrupulous exactnefs in that operation, and he perfectly feconded my intentions.

During this time, my indefatigable friend, William Thornton, took a drawing of the cave, which could be feen in a true point of view from the fea only. This task was neither agreeable nor free from danger; for it required all the addrefs of our feamen to keep him for a few moments in front of the entrance, amidft the whirlpools and waves of a fea which feemed eager to devour the frail skiff. It was neceffary to return inceffantly

to

to the fame point, and to give reft at intervals to my dear Thornton, who became fick with her rolling.

Our ardour and perfeverance were unfhaken, and nothing was capable of diftracting our attention. We only looked abroad, from time to time, to fee whether the fea was likely to be equally favourable during the remainder of the day. After noting down all the particulars of the cave of Fingal, after sketching fuch objects as moft interefted us, and taking the dimenfions which I was very happy to obtain, I ftill proceeded to examine fome other parts of the ifland; and I made a collection of different lavas, zeolites, and other ftones, tending to illuftrate the natural hiftory of the place.

I faw with fome uneafinefs that the fun was now about to leave us, and that it became neceffary to withdraw from a place which prefented fcenes fo attractive and volcanic phœnomena fo remarkable. But the weather might change in a moment, and we had a long paffage to make; we therefore prepared for our departure. We embarked at half paft four in the afternoon, and took some refreshment on our way, for we were almost starving with hunger. Our indefatigable Hebridians, who felt neither our curiosity nor our taste, except so far as respected the cave of Fingal, for which they entertain a sacred veneration, had made a hearty repast on the island, and diminished the weight of our stores, while we were occupied in seeing and observing every thing. They were quite contented, and rowed us along with a spirit and vigour, which were at once a proof of their strength and of their habitual capacity for toil. They were completely enraptured with the prospect of carrying us back safe and sound, owing to the fineness of the day and the calmness of the sea. They accordingly continued their songs till our arrival at nine o'clock at the castle of Torloisk, where the good Mr. M'Lean, his family, and our friends, were impatiently expecting us.

I employed myself during several days in digesting my observations on the isle of Staffa; and for the sake of greater method and perspicuity, I thought proper to adopt the following order. The reader will be
pleased

pleafed to recollect that this defcription is principally intended for fuch as employ themfelves in the natural hiftory of ftones and minerals. If it be confidered as rather tedious by thofe who are not attached to that ftudy, it will be eafy for them to pafs on to other fubjects.

CHAPTER IV.

Description and Natural History of the Isle of Staffa.—General Views.

THE isle of Staffa is situated in the fifty-seventh degree of north latitude, and fifteen miles west of the island of Mull. Its form is oblong and irregular. Its coasts are steep and craggy, surrounded with superb basaltic causeways, and hollowed into different caves, such as those of Fingal and the *Corvorant*. The isle is accessible only by a small opening or entrance, where the precipice sinks into a slope, but which can admit only a small boat, and that in the calmest weather; for if there be the smallest breeze, it becomes dangerous to attempt landing, and the boat is obliged to take shelter in the island of Iona.

The total circumference of Staffa is little more than two miles. The most elevated part of the isle is over the cave of Fingal, where it is one hundred and fourteen feet above the level of the sea in ordinary tides.

The

Designed by E. Tond.

View of the Isle of Staffa, from the North West.

I. King sculp.

The sides of this vast rock are entirely bare; the waves and currents batter and undermine them every where. There is on the most elevated part only, a flat piece of ground covered with a thin dry turf, contiguous to which is a small spot but newly broke up, where a little oats and a few potatoes are raised. It has also a small pasturage and a scanty spring, which would be soon dried up, were it not that the climate is so rainy.

There is neither tree nor bush to be seen; and for firing, the inhabitants are obliged to make use of a bad sod, which they cut in the summer season in order to dry it. It cannot be called peat; for it consists simply of the fibrous roots of common grass, intermixed with earth. It would be impossible to find a worse fewel; but here necessity reigns with absolute sway.

The whole of the isle belongs to Colonel Charles Campbell, of Cambeltown, in Cantyre. It is let at the rent of twelve pounds sterling; on account, probably, of its fishery, for its territorial value ought to be considered as nothing.

The total population, at the time when I viſited it, confiſted only of two families, who lived apart in two huts, conſtructed of rude blocks of baſaltes, roofed over with ſods, and who amounted, men, women, and children, to the number of ſixteen*. Belonging to theſe, there were eight cows, one bull, twelve wethers or ſheep, two horſes, one hog, two dogs, eight hens, and one cock.

Buchanan has ſlightly mentioned the iſle of Staffa and its remarkable columns. But Sir Joſeph Banks, Preſident of the Royal Society of London, is the firſt who examined this grand and aſtoniſhing object of natural hiſtory with the eye of an obſerver. It has riſen into celebrity by his deſcription of it, which was publiſhed in the Tour to the Hebrides, by Thomas Pennant, accompanied with plates.

---

* At the time when Sir Joſeph Banks, in 1772, viſited this iſland, along with ſeveral naturaliſts, of whom Mr. Troil was one, it belonged to Mr. Lauchlan M'Quaire, and it had only a ſingle inhabitant.

" There is only one hut," ſays Mr. Troil, " which is
" occupied by a peaſant, who attends ſome cattle that
" paſture there. To teſtify his joy for our arrival, he
" ſung all night over in the Earſe language, which we did
" not underſtand. He regaled us with fiſh and with
" milk."—*Letters on Iceland*, by Troil, Archbiſhop of Linckœping.

Mr.

Mr. Troïl, bifhop of Linckœping, one of Sir Jofeph Banks's fellow-travellers, has given a defcription of the fame ifle, and of the cave of Fingal, in a learned and curious work upon Iceland*. But as thefe two travellers have principally attended to the picturefque fcenes, without entering into thofe details which are more particularly interefting to naturalifts, I conceived that it would give fatisfaction to fome perfons that I fhould purfue the latter track.

OF THE CAVE OF FINGAL, OR AN-UA-VINE.

This fuperb monument of a grand fubterraneous combuftion, the date of which has been loft in the lapfe of ages, prefents an appearance of order and regularity fo wonderful, that it is difficult for the coldeft obferver, and one the leaft fenfible to the phœnomena which relate to the convulfions of the globe,

---

* This work, written in the Swedifh language, has been tranflated into French by M. De Lindholm, and printed at Paris by Didot 1781, in 1 vol. 8vo. with plates. It were to be wifhed that the tranflator, to whom the Sciences are indebted for rendering that excellent book into our language, had been more acquainted with natural hiftory; his notes would then have more intereft, and contain fewer errors.

not

not to be singularly astonished by this prodigy, which may be considered as a kind of natural palace.

To shelter myself from all critical observation on the emotions which I experienced while contemplating the most extraordinary of any cavern known, I shall borrow the expressions of him who first described it. Those who are acquainted with the character of this illustrious naturalist, will not be apt to accuse him of being liable to be hurried away by the force of a too ardent imagination; but the sensation which he felt at the view of this magnificent scene was such, that it was impossible to escape a degree of just enthusiasm.

" The impatience which every body felt to
" see the wonders we had heard so largely de-
" scribed, prevented our morning's rest; every
" one was up and in motion before the break of
" day, and with the first light arrived at the
" S. W. part of the island, the seat of the most
" remarkable pillars; where we no sooner ar-
" rived than we were struck with a scene of
" magnificence which exceeded our expecta-
" tion, though formed as we thought upon
" the most sanguine foundations: The whole
" of that end of the island, supported by
" ranges

" ranges of natural pillars, moftly above
" fifty feet high, ftanding in natural colo-
" nades, according as the bays or points of
" lands formed themfelves ; upon a firm bafis
" of folid unformed rock. In a fhort time
" we arrived at the mouth of the cave, the
" moft magnificent, I fuppofe, that has ever
" been defcribed by travellers. . . . .

" The mind can hardly form an idea more
" magnificent than fuch a fpace, fupported
" on each fide by ranges of columns, and
" roofed by the bottoms of thofe that have
" been broke off in order to form it; be-
" tween the angles of which a yellow ftalag-
" mitic matter has exu'd, which ferves to
" define the angles precifely, and at the
" fame time vary the colour with a great
" deal of elegance ; and to render it ftill
" more agreeable, the whole is lighted from
" without; fo that the fartheft extremity is
" very plainly feen from without, and the
" air within being agitated by the flux and
" reflux of the tides, is perfectly dry and
" wholefome, free entirely from the damp
" vapours with which natural caverns in ge-
" neral abound."

Let

Let us alfo, for a moment, liften to Mr. Troil upon the fame fubject.

"How fplendid," fays this prelate, "do the porticos of the ancients appear in our eyes, from the oftentatious magnificence of the defcriptions we have received of them, and with what admiration are we feized on feeing even the colonades of our modern edifices! But when we behold the cave of Fingal, formed by nature, in the ifle of Staffa, it is no longer poffible to make a comparifon, and we are forced to acknowledge that this piece of architecture, executed by nature, far furpaffes that of the Louvre, that of St. Peter at Rome, and even what remains of Palmira and Peftum, and all that the genius, the tafte, and the luxury of the Greeks, were ever capable of inventing *."

Such was the impreffion made by the cave of Fingal on Sir Jofeph Banks, and on the bifhop of Linckœping. I have feen many ancient volcanos, and I have given defcriptions of feveral fuperb bafaltic caufeways and delightful caverns in the midft of lavas. But

---

* Letters on Iceland, by Mr. Troil.

I have

I have never found any thing which comes near this, or can bear any comparifon with it, either for the admirable regularity of the columns, the height of the arch, the fituation, the forms, the elegance of this production of nature, or its refemblance to the mafter-pieces of art: though this has had no fhare in its conftruction. It is therefore not at all furprifing that tradition fhould have made it the abode of a hero.

This charming monument of nature is thirty-five feet wide at the entrance, fifty-fix feet high, and a hundred and forty feet long.

The upright columns which compofe the frontifpiece, are of the moft perfect regularity. Their height to the beginning of the curvature is forty-five feet.

The arch is compofed of two unequal fegments of a circle, which form a fort of natural pediment.

The mafs which crowns, or rather which forms, the roof, is twenty feet thick in its loweft part. It confifts of fmall prifms, more or lefs regular, inclining in all directions, clofely united and cemented underneath and in the joints with a yellowifh white calcareous matter, and fome zeolitic infiltrations, which give

give this fine ceiling the appearance of mofaic work.

The fea reaches to the very extremity of the cave. It is fifteen feet deep at the mouth; and its waves, inceffantly agitated, beat with great noife againft the bottom and walls of the cavern, and every where break into foam. The light alfo penetrates through its whole length, diminifhing gradually inwards, and exhibiting the moft wonderful varieties of colour.

The right fide of the entrance prefents, on its exterior part, a vaft amphitheatre, formed of different ranges of large truncated prifms, the top of which may be eafily walked along. Several of thefe prifms are jointed, that is, concave on the one fide, and convex on the other; and fome of them are divided by fimple tranfverfe interfections*.

Thefe prifms, confifting of a very durable and pure black bafaltes, are from one to three feet in diameter. Their forms are

* Sir Jofeph Banks's draughtfman, very good and accurate in other refpects, has fubftituted, probably to give greater effect to the cave, large maffes of ftone irregularly piled on each other, on the right fide of the kind of amphitheatre, which ferves as a bafis to that part of the grove. But there is in reality nothing there except columns.

trian-

triangular, tetrahedial, pentagonal, and hexagonal; and some of them have seven or eight sides. I saw several large prisms on the truncatures, of which are distinctly traced the outlines of a number of smaller prisms; that is, these prisms are formed of a basaltes, which has a tendency to subdivide itself likewise into prisms. I had before observed the same phenomenon in the basaltic prisms of Vivarais.

The cave can be entered only by proceeding along the platform on the right side, which I have mentioned above. But the way grows very narrow and difficult as it advances; for this sort of interior gallery, raised about fifteen feet above the level of the sea, is formed entirely of truncated perpendicular prisms of a great or less height, between which considerable address is necessary to choose one's steps, the passages being sometimes so strait and so slippery, owing to the droppings from the roof, that I took the very prudent resolution, suggested by our two guides, to proceed barefooted, and to take advantage of their assistance, especially in a particular place, where I had room only to plant one foot, whilst I clung with my right hand

hand to a large prifm to fupport myfelf, and held the hand of one of the guides by the other. This difficult operation took place at the darkeft part of the cave; and one half of the body was at the time fufpended over an abyfs, where the fea dafhed itfelf into a cloud of foam.

I was defirous of penetrating to the fartheft extremity, and I accomplifhed my purpofe, though not without confiderable difficulty and danger. I, more than once, found my attention diftracted from the obfervations which I was happy to have an opportunity of making, to the thought of how I fhould get back again.

As I drew near the bottom of the cave, the bold balcony, on which I walked, expanded into a large floping fpace compofed of thoufands of broken vertical columns. The bottom was bounded by a compact range of pillars of unequal height, and refembling the front of an organ.

It is worthy of remark, that at the time when Mr. Troil vifited the cave, the fea, by one of thofe uncommon chances which do not happen once in ten years, was fo calm that it permitted him to enter with a boat.

" At

"At the very bottom of the cave," says Mr. Troil, " and a little above the surface of the water there is a kind of small cave which sends forth a very agreeable noise every time that the water rushes into it *."

As the sea was far from being completely still, when I visited it, I heard a noise of a very different nature every time that the waves, in rapid succession, broke against its bottom. This sound resembled that which is produced by striking a large hard body with great weight and force against another hard body in a subterraneous cavity. The shock was so violent that it was heard at some distance, and the whole cavern seemed to shake with it. Being close to the place whence the sound issued, and where the water is not so deep upon the retreat of the wave, I endeavoured to discover the cause of this terrible collision. I soon observed, that, a little below the basis which supported the organ-fronted colonade, there was an aperture which formed the outlet of a hollow, or perhaps a small cave. It was impossible to penetrate into this cavity, but it may be pre-

---

* Letters on Iceland.

fumed that the tremendous noife was occafioned by a broken rock, driven by the violent impetuofity of the furge againft its fides. By the boiling motion of the water, however, in the fame place, it is evident that there are feveral other fmall paffages, through which it iffues, after rufhing into the principal aperture in a mafs. It is therefore not impoffible, when the fea is not fufficiently agitated, to put the emprifoned rock in motion, that the air, ftrongly compreffed by the weight of the water, which is in inceffant fluctuation, fhould, on rufhing out by the fmall lateral paffages, produce a particular ftrange found. It might then be truly regarded as an organ created by the hand of Nature; and this circumftance would fully explain why the ancient and real name of this cave in the Earfe language is, *the melodious cave**.

Sir

---

* Sir Jofeph Banks is the firft who gave the cave of Staffa the name of the cave of Fingal. I made the moft minute enquiries of feveral perfons well fkilled in the Earfe, Gaulic, or Celtic language, to know what relation this cave had to the father of Offian. And thefe gentlemen, as well as others, affured me, that the miftake was owing to the name being equivocal. The following is their explanation: The true name of the cave is *un-ua-vine*. *An*, the; *ua*, grotto, cave, cavern; *vine*, melodious. The name of Fingal in the fame language is fpelled and pronounced

Sir Joseph Banks in the description which he has given us of the cave of Staffa, says, that " between the angles a yellow stalag- " mitic matter has exuded, which seemed to " define the angles precisely." That is true, but the learned Naturalist has not told us the nature of this yellowish matter.

Mr. Troil mentions it also: He says, that " the colour of the columns is a dark grey; " but that the joints are filled with a quart- " rose stalactites, which distinctly marks the " separation of the columns, and which, by " the variety of its tints, has the most agree- " able effect on the eye." There is certainly an error here with regard to the substance. On breaking off several pieces of it, which it is not very easy to do, owing to the height of

nounced *Fion* in the nominative. But the Earse nouns are declinable, and the genitive of Fingal is *Fine*; so that if one wished to express the cave of Fingal in the Earse language, he would write *an-ua-fine*. Thus between the Earse *vine* melodious, and the genitive of Fingal *fine*, there is no other difference than the change of the letter *v* into *f*; and some person not very well versed in the Earse language, might have translated to Sir Joseph Banks the words *au-ua-vine* by the *cave of Fingal*, whilst the true and literal interpretation is, the *melodious cave*. In this cafe, the observation of Mr. Troil, on the agreeable sound which he heard issuing from the bottom of the cave when the water rushed in, is valuable, and comes in support of the true denomination.

the

the vault, I found that it was nothing but a calcareous matter coloured by the decompofition of the iron of the lava, and intermixed with a little argillaceous earth. This ftalactites has alfo very little adhefion, and is in general of an earthy nature. In feveral of the prifms I found fome globules of zeolites, but in very fmall quantity. I alfo broke off from between two prifms, which were fo far apart as to admit of introducing my hand, an incruftation in which the white and tranfparent zeolites was formed into very perfect fmall cubical cryftals, feveral of which were coloured red by the ferruginous lime arifing from the decompofition of the lava. But I muft repeat, that zeolites is very rare in this cave, and having myfelf broken off all the fpecimens that I was able to fee, I doubt whether thofe who may vifit the place after me will find any quantity of it.

DIMENSIONS OF THE CAVE OF FINGAL.

Breadth of the entrance, taken at the mouth and at the level of the fea, 35 feet.

Height from the level of the fea to the pitch of the arch, 56 feet.

Depth

Depth of the sea, oppofite to the entrance, and twelve feet diftant from it, at noon of the 27th of September, fifteen feet.

Thicknefs of the roof meafured from the pitch of the arch without to its higheft part, twenty feet.

Interior length of the cave from the entrance to the extremity, one hundred and forty feet.

Height of the talleft columns on the right fide of the entrance, forty-five feet.

Depth of the fea in the interior part of the cave, ten feet nine inches; in fome places eight feet, and towards the bottom fomewhat lefs*.

I have given a defcription of the largeft cave, as it is at the fame time the moft remarkable. But there is another towards the northern part of the ifland, in the midft of a fine

* All the dimenfions were taken with great exactnefs with a piece of thread-tape, painted and waxed, divided into French toifes, feet and inches, and rolling up into a leather cafe. This inftrument, which I caufed to be made in London, afforded a meafure of 100 feet. If I, therefore, differ in the leaft from the dimenfions taken by Sir Jofeph Banks, attention muft be had to the difference of the Englifh foot. This naturalift, befides, ufed a fifhing line, which, ftretching more or lefs with the wet, can never give the meafures fufficiently correct.

colonade. Its name in the Earfe language is *Oua-na-Scarve.* It is, however, lefs interefting than the firft, and was befides inacceffible at the time I vifited the ifland. There is alfo in the fouthern quarter, and at a fhort diftance from the place where we difembarked, a fmall cave compofed of compact lava, furmounted with a range of prifms, the total appearance of which, as is obferved by Sir Jofeph Banks, exactly refembles the keel of a veffel having her timbers expofed to view. The curvature of the prifms renders the refemblance of this fingular fpectacle very ftriking.

More than one half the circumference of the ifle is occupied by very handfome colonades, which are completely bare on the fide next the fea. They reft in general on a current of gravelly lava, which ferves for their bafis and fupport; and they follow the direction more or lefs inclined, more or lefs horizontal of the current. All thefe prifmatic caufeways are covered with a vaft ftream of lava, more or lefs compact, and tending more or lefs to a prifmatic form. The fummit of this covering is fpead over with a little vegetable earth formed by decompofed lava, and with fome thin common grafs.

Above

Above one half the ifland therefore is fupported by columns more or lefs perpendicular, and the remaining part entirely confifts of lavas more or lefs compact, more or lefs decompofed, more or lefs intermixed with fragments of other lavas, zeolitic infiltrations, calcareous ftreaks, and calcedonious droppings, which have in fome places penetrated the fubftance of the zeolites.

One of the caufeways to the northward of the grand cave merits the attention of the naturalift by the difpofition, the number, the purity, and elevation of the prifms, which are more than forty-eight feet high, and placed perpendicularly like the pipes of an organ. This magnificent colonade is fpread over with a current of compact lava, more than fifty feet thick, and compofed of innumerable fmall prifms which diverge in all directions. It is fupported by a current of black gravelly lava, nine feet thick, the pafte of which is an intermixture of different other lavas divided into fmall irregular fragments, and united by a natural cement, compofed of calcareous earth, zeolites, and a calcedonious fubftance. Every thing leads me to regard this current as the refult of a volcanic eruption, in which the water entering into concourſe with fire, has mixed all theſe matters in one paſte. A part of this current of lava extends under the ſea.

To prevent my deſcription from becoming too tedious, I ſhall now only ſay a few words reſpecting what is improperly called the iſle of *Boo-ſha-la*; improperly, becauſe the name of iſle can never be given to what evidently forms an appendage of the principal iſle.

Boo-ſha-la lies at a ſmall diſtance from the grand cave, and is ſeparated from Staffa by a channel which is only a few fathoms wide; its junction with the latter may be eaſily traced in the ſea. Boo-ſha-la itſelf ſeems to be divided into two parts at ſpring tides. It is compoſed of a number of banks of priſmatic baſaltes of a very pure kind, piled together in ſome places, arched in others, and ſometimes diſpoſed in the manner of ſteps, which form a paſſable, though ſteep ſtair-caſe. By the ſide of this the columns are vertical, and form by their union and their different degrees of elevation, a regular conic peak, which is entirely an aſſemblage of priſms. This remarkable ſtructure is not owing to the falling of large maſſes from their former poſitions.

It

SECTION V of the STRATA, to the LOW MAIN COAL,
At S.t Anthon's Colliery
near Newcastle upon Tyne.
The Property of George Johnson Esq.r & C.o

Strata	Fath.s	Feet	In.s
Soil & Clay	5		
Brown Freestone	12		
Coal			
Blue Metal Stone	2	5	
White Girdles	2	1	
Coal			8
White & Grey Freestone	6		
Soft Blue Metal Stone	5		
Coal			6
Freestone Girdles	3		
Whin	1	4	6
Strong Freestone	3	1	
Coal			1
Soft Blue Thill	1	3	
Soft Girdles mixed with Whin	3	5	
Coal			6
Blue & Black Stone	3	3	
Coal	1		8
Strong Freestone		3	
Grey Metal Stone	1	4	8
Coal			
Grey Post mixed with Whin	4	1	
Grey Girdles	3	1	
Blue & Black Stone	2	2	
Coal			1
Grey Metal Stone	2		
Strong Freestone	6		
Black Metal Stone with hard Girdles	3		
HIGH MAIN COAL			
Grey Metal	70 / 4	3	
Post Girdles		2/4	8
Girdles			
Blue Metal Stone	5		
Post	3	1	
Blue Metal Stone	3	1	6
Whin & Blue Metal			
Strong Freestone	3	3	
Brown Post with Water			7
Blue Metal Stone with Grey Girdles	2	2	
Coal		3	
Blue Metal Stone	3	3	3
Freestone		4	
Strong Grey Metal with Post Girdles	7	4	8
Strong Freestone	2	4	
Blue Metal Stone	1/2	4	7
Grey Metal Stone with Post Girdles	2	4	5
Blue Metal Stone with Whin Girdles	1	3	3/4
Coal			3/4
Blue Grey Metal		3	7
Freestone	2		
Freestone mixed with Whin			
Freestone	1	2	
Blue Metal & Coal	2	2	8
Grey Metal Stone & Girdles			
Freestone mixed with Whin	3	1	7
Whin			
Freestone mixed with Whin			
Grey Metal Stone			10
Grey Metal & Whin Girdles			
Grey Metal & Girdles	1		
Freestone			8
Grey & Whin Metal			9
Blue & Grey Metal	2		
Freestone mixed with Whin			8
Grey Metal			8
Grey Metal & Girdles	1		
LOW MAIN COAL			
Total	135	1	0

A Scale of FATHOMS

Boring Pit 135 Fathoms

It feems rather to be the effect of a more or lefs gradual cooling; and the matter in fhrinking appears to have undergone thofe fantaftic modifications and accidents, which may be obferved in cryftallizations on a large fcale; though I am far from confidering the prifmatic lava as the refult of cryftallization. On the contrary, I reject that opinion; and the comparifon which I ufe here is only for the purpofe of making myfelf more intelligible, and has no relation but to the accidental varieties and different difpofitions of the forms.

Mr. Thomas Pennant has publifhed, in his Tour to the Hebrides, two engavings of Boo-fha-la, taken from the very correct drawings of Mr. Banks.

It remains only that I fhould give a lift of the lithological productions of the ifle of Staffa.

MINERALOGY OF THE ISLE OF STAFFA.

1. Triangular bafaltic prifms, which are here, as in other places, very rare.
2. Quadrangular, and equally rare.
3. Pentagonal: ⎫ Thefe are the moft
4. Exagonal: ⎭ common forms.
5. Hepta-

5. Heptagonal, of which a few are found here.

6. Octogonal, of a large fize, fometimes four feet in diameter, exhibiting in their truncatures the elements of other fmaller prifms.

7. Articulated prifms, that is, whofe fections are concave on one fide and convex on the other.

8. Prifms cut ftraight without any articulations, fome of them have eight, ten, and even twelve fections.

9. Prifms which feem to have been caft at one time, in one piece; of thefe, fome are twelve, fifteen, twenty, and even forty feet high.

10. Prifms curved in an arch of a circle.

11. Black gravelly compact lava, which eafily feparates into irregular pieces.

12. Black porous lava. The extinguifhed volcano, in the ifle of Staffa, has been expofed for fo many ages to the fury of a fea full of currents, and agitated with tempefts, that it may well be faid to have left only the skeleton of a volcanic ifle, much more confiderable in former times; the fea which attacks it on every fide having carried away or de-

ftroyed

stroyed every thing that it was capable of acting upon. It ought not, therefore, to be a subject of wonder, that it contains neither the remains of a crater, nor scoriæ, nor light lavas. The same thing has happened to other extinct volcanos which the sea abandoned, after an incalculable lapse of ages. On examining, however, with attention the substances which compose the currents of lava, which support many of the prismatic causeways of the isle, one discovers some fragments of a black porous lava. These lavas being mixed and intersperfed among the fragments of other lavas, compact, pulverulent or gravelly, compressed by the enormous weight of the superior masses, and united by a gluten, partly calcareous and partly zeolitic, are thence more protected from the action of the waves.

13. White radiated zeolites, incrusted with basaltic lava. The same zeolites incrusted with black lava, much softer, in round pieces, oval or irregular, and in diverging points. There are sometimes seen on the exterior part of these oval pieces, projecting crystals of cubical zeolites.

14. White

14. White radiated calcedonious zeolites. I obtained from one of the beds of muddy lava, on which the greater part of the prifmatic lavas of Staffa repofe, feveral fpherical nuclei of zeolites in diverging rays, united to the number of three or four in one group. Several of thefe fmall balls were completely folvable in the nitrous acid, with which they formed a jelly; whilft feveral others adhering to thefe, but femi-tranfparent and of an unctuous polifh, were impervious to the acid, and even gave fparks with fteel. But on calcining and reducing the latter to powder, and digefting them in a glafs veffel with nitrous acid in a fand bath, the acid diffolves the zeolites and forms a jelly with it, whilft the calcedonious particles remaining untouched, are precipitated to the bottom. I found fome of thefe fmall balls of the fize of a gall-nut, the one half of which was penetrated by a calcedonious milky juice, and the other by a quartzofe juice extremely cryftalline, and as tranfparent as the pureft rock cryftal.

15. Cubical white zeolites. There were fome of the moft fuperb pieces of cubical zeolites

lites in Staffa; but, in our vifit to that ifle, we took away all that were moft interefting. Before us, doctor Thompfon had alfo made at Staffa a very interefting collection of zeolites, and among others, a number of large cubic cryftals joined together on a black compact lava. This fpecimen, the moft confiderable and the moft perfect of its kind, may be feen at Oxford in the collection of that naturalift.

16. Tranfparent cubical zeolites, of a greenifh caft. I found this fpecimen in the interior of the cave of Fingal, in a crevice formed by the feparation of two prifms. It is therefore very evident that this fmall group of cubical cryftals had been formed in that fiffure in a very flow and infenfible manner, by the juxta-pofition of the zeolitic particles held in folution by the aqueous fluid. The greenifh colour of the latter zeolites is owing to the decompofition of the iron contained in the bafaltes.

17. White femi-tranfparent zeolites in octagonal cryftals.

18. White femi-tranfparent zeolites in cryftals of thirty facettes.

Such are the moft remarkable zeolites which I have found in the ifle of Staffa. It

is

is not improbable that the waves and currents which daily wear away its coafts may afterwards difcover fome other varieties.

19. Granite of a red ground, and of the fame texture with that of the ancient Egyptian granite, but of a much lefs vivid colour. This red granite is found in rounded ftones of a pretty large fize among the rolled lavas thrown by the fea upon that part of the ifland where the currents have formed the moft confiderable breach. As every thing in Staffa is completely volcanic, it is evident that thefe blocks of granite, which are not very abundant, but which have been rounded by friction, have been tranfported from a diftance by currents; for the neighbouring iflands are equally volcanic. The fea muft certainly be terribly agitated to raife thefe rounded granites to the height at which they are found on the ifle of Staffa, among the bafaltic lavas equally rounded, which the fea throws up during fpring tides and furious tempefts.

CHAP.

CHAPTER V.

Stay at Mr. M'Lean's.—Cuſtoms and Manners of the Inhabitants of the Iſle of Mull.

MR. M'LEAN of Torloiſk has erected a commodious habitation, in the modern ſtile, but without any parade. Its characteriſtic is an exquiſite neatneſs, joined to the moſt attractive ſimplicity.

It commands a view of the ſea, and the iſles of Ulva, Gommetra, Staffa, Iona, and numerous cluſters of rocks, which render navigation ſo dangerous in that region.

This houſe is ſituated on a ſingle flat eminence, deſtitute of trees and verdure; ſo that to form a ſmall kitchen garden, Mr. M'Lean has been obliged to dig away part of the volcanic rock, and fill up the area with tranſported ſoil; he ſhewed me ſeveral difficult and expenſive operations of this kind which he had executed. On my aſking, why he ſuffered to remain ſtanding upon the place a kind of large cottage built of dry ſtones, covered with ſtraw, or rather heath, and lighted by by two narrow holes, which fcarcely admitted the rays of the fun.

"It was there," faid Mr. M'Lean with emotion, "that I was born. That is the "ancient habitation of my fathers; and I feel "unexpreffible regard for this modeft manfion, "which reminds me of their virtues and "frugal life." This reply more ftrongly marks the character of that eftimable man than the moft eloquent defcription which I could give. It ought to be remarked, that Mr. M'Lean is a man of birth and fortune, that he has ferved in the Britifh army, performed diftant voyages, and is well acquainted with the world. He has, notwithftanding, preferred his native foil, and an agricultural life, to a refidence in London or Edinburgh, or the moft fertile plains of England; fo powerful is the dominion of our firft habits, when it recals to our minds the indelible pleafures of infancy.

Several ladies from Edinburgh, of agreeable converfation, were at Torloifk at the fame time with me. One of them, a relation of the Melforts, of whom there is a branch fettled in France, was a woman of talents and information. A young officer, nephew to Mr.

Mr. M'Lean, and two of his friends, were also on a visit at Torloisk; where all were united in the delightful bonds of confidence and friendship.

Miss M'Lean was an only daughter, of a pleasing countenance, elegant figure, and highly interesting from her talents, her acquirements, and her modesty. She played extremely well upon the harpsicord, and was in every respect the charm of that happy society. She had attentively studied the language, poetry, and music of the Hebridians.

Miss M'Lean assured me, in several conversations, with which she favoured me upon the subject, that to one acquainted with the language, the usages, and the manners of the country, it was difficult to conceive how the English writers, who were utter strangers to the Celtic tongue, should have so obstinately persisted in doubting the existence of the ancient poems of Ossian. She admitted, that they are in many places incomplete, and in others altered; for it cannot be supposed that they have not sustained some loss in their transmission from bard to bard, and from one generation to another. But it is nevertheless true, that several pieces of them have come

come down entire, accompanied with some remains of the music to which they have been sung. This music is indeed wild and rude when compared to ours, but possesses the most powerful charms for the Highlanders, by calling to their minds the combats, victories, loves, and illustrious actions of their heroic ancestors.

No one is more capable of converting those who are incredulous upon this point than Miss M'Lean, and I invite her in the name of the sister arts, of poetry and music, with which she is so well acquainted, to publish her researches respecting the poems and airs of the ancient Caledonians *.

Mr. M'Lean's domestics, both men and women, are clothed in the Hebridian mode.

---

* Besides what M'Pherson has said upon the subject, John Smith, minister of Kilbrundon in Argyleshire, has written in favour of the authenticity of the poems of Ossian, Ullin, Onan, &c. Mr. Nichol, of Lifemore, has also treated the same subject. John Clarke, of Edinburgh, has given a translation of several of the Caledonian bards. I purchased also at Edinburgh a collection of Galic music, published by a presbyterian minister, and several other printed and manuscript pieces relative to this question; which I can communicate to such as it particularly interests. But this great question being foreign to the principal object of my researches, I shall forbear to expatiate upon it in this place.

I have

ENGLAND AND SCOTLAND. 67

I have already defcribed the drefs of the men, in mentioning the inhabitants of Dalmally. That of the women is much lefs complex. Their long flowing hair, which is in general black, forms the only ornament of their heads. Some indeed have it kept back with a fimple woollen fillet ftriped of different colours, among which red and green are invariably predominant. From one article of expence they are entirely free: they wear neither fhoes nor ftockings. But notwithftanding the length of the winter, and the inceffant humidity of the climate, and though they go with their heads bare, their teeth do not feem to be in the leaft affected. Their drefs confifts of a bodice, or rather a kind of veft, and a, petticoat of a woollen ftuff chequered with red, green and brown ftripes, fhaded with blue. This is the general and favourite clothing of the Highlanders, and is ufed alike by the men and women, though it is for the moft part manufactured in the fouthern parts of Scotland. It is known by the name of *Tartan.*

The Englifh eat very little bread; the Scots eat more: there were three different kinds ufed at Mr. M'Lean's table.

The

The firſt, which may be regarded as a luxury for the country, is ſea biſcuit, which veſſels from Glaſgow ſometimes leave in paſſing.

The ſecond is made of oatmeal formed into an unleavened dough, and then ſpread with a rolling pin into round cakes, about a foot in diameter and the twelfth part of an inch thick. Theſe cakes are baked, or rather dried, on a thin plate of iron which is ſuſpended over the fire. This is the principal bread of ſuch as are in eaſy circumſtances.

The third kind, which is ſpecially appropriated to tea and breakfaſt, in the opulent families of the iſles, conſiſts of barley cakes, without leaven, and prepared in the ſame manner as the preceding, but ſo thin, that after ſpreading them over with butter, they are eaſily doubled into ſeveral folds; which render them very agreeable to thoſe who are fond of this kind of dainties.

At ten in the morning, the bell announces that breakfaſt is on the table. All repair to the parlour, where they find a fire of peat, mixed with pit-coal, and a table elegantly ſerved up and covered with the following articles :—

Plates.

Plates of fmoaked beef,
Cheefe of the country and Englifh cheefe, in
trays of mahogany,
Frefh eggs,
Salted herring,
Butter,
Milk and cream,
A fort of *bouillie*, of oatmeal and water. In
eating this *bouillie*, each fpoonful is plunged
into a bafon of cream, which is always
befide it.
Milk worked up with the yolks of eggs,
fugar and rum. This fingular mixture is
drank cold, and without being prepared
by fire :
Current jelly,
Conferve of myrtle, a wild fruit that grows
among the heath,
Tea,
Coffee,
The three forts of bread above-mentioned;
and, Jamaica Rum.

Such is the ftyle in which Mr. M'Lean's
breakfaft-table was ferved up every morning,
while we were at his houfe. There was always the fame abundance, with no other difference

ference in general than in the greater or lefs variety of the difhes *.

Dinner is put on the table at four o'clock. It confifts in general of the following particulars, which I correctly noted in my journal.

1. A large difh of Scotch foup, compofed of broth of beef, mutton, and fometimes fowl, mixed with a little oatmeal, onions, parfley, and a confiderable quantity of peafe. Inftead of flices of bread, as in France, fmall flices of mutton and the giblets of fowls are thrown into this foup.

---

* Knox, who travelled more upon the main land than in the iflands, gives the following particulars of the breakfafts of the more wealthy families:—
 "A dram of whiskey, gin, rum, or brandy, plain or
 " infufed with berries that grow among the heath; French
 " rolls; oat and barley bread; tea and coffee; honey in the
 " comb, red and black current jellies; marmalade, con-
 " ferves and excellent cream; fine flavoured butter,
 " frefh and falted; Chefhire and Highland cheefe, the laft
 " very indifferent; a plateful of very frefh eggs; frefh and
 " falted herrings broiled; ditto, haddocks and whitings,
 " the skin being taken off; cold round of venifon, beef
 " and mutton hams. Befides thefe articles, which are
 " commonly placed on the table at once, there are gene-
 " rally cold beef and moor-fowl to thofe who choofe to
 " call for them. After breakfaft, the men amufe them-
 " felves with the gun, fifhing, or failing, till the evening;
 " when they dine, which meal ferves with fome families
 " for fupper."

2. Pudding

2. Pudding of bullock's blood and barley meal, seasoned with plenty of pepper and ginger.
3. Excellent beef-steaks broiled.
4. Roasted mutton of the best quality.
5. Potatoes done in the juice of the mutton.
6. Sometimes heath-cocks, wood-cocks or water-fowl.
7. Cucumbers and ginger pickled with vinegar.
8. Milk prepared in a variety of ways.
9. Cream and Madeira wine.
10. Pudding made of barley-meal, cream, and currants of Corinth, done up with suet.

All these various dishes appear on the table at the same time; the mistress of the house presides, and serves all round.

In a very short time the toasts commence; it is the business of the mistress to begin the ceremony. A large glass filled with port-wine is put into her hand; she drinks to the health of all the company, and passes it to one of the persons who sit next to her; and it thus proceeds from one to another round the whole table.

The side-board is furnished with three large glasses of a similar kind; of which one is appropriated

propriated to beer, another to wine, and the third to water, when it is called for in its unmixed ftate, which is not often. Thefe glaffes are common to all at table ; they are never rinfed, but merely wiped with a fine towel after each perfon drinks.

The deffert, from the want of fruit, confifts for the moft part, only of two forts of cheefe, that of Chefhire, and what is made in the country itfelf.

The cloth is removed after the deffert, and a table of well polifhed mahogany, appears in all its luftre. It is foon covered with elegant glafs decanters of Englifh manufacture, containing port, cherry, and Madeira wines, and with capacious bowls filled with punch. Small glaffes are then profufely diftributed to every one.

In England, the ladies leave table the moment the toafts begin. The cuftom is not precifely the fame here; they remain at leaft half an hour after, and juftly partake in the feftivity of a fcene, in which formality being laid afide, Scottifh franknefs and kindnefs have full room to difplay themfelves. It is certain that the men are benefited by this intercoufe, and the ladies are nothing the lofers by it.

At

At Mr. M'Lean's we drank in particular to each of the ladies prefent.

To the reft of the guefts, mentioning their names one by one.

To the country.

To liberty.

To the happinefs of mankind in general.

To friendfhip.

We, foreigners, drank more than once to our good friends the Highlanders; and the company anfwered in full chorus with drinking to our friends in France, and in a lower tone, with a glafs of mild Madeira, to our miftreffes.

The ladies then left us for a little to prepare the tea. They returned in about half an hour after; and the fervants followed them with coffee, fmall tarts, butter, milk, and tea. Mufic, converfation, reading the news, though a little old by the time they reach this, and walking, when the weather permits, fill up the remainder of the evening; and thus the time paffes quickly away. But it is fomewhat unpleafant to be obliged to take one's feat at table again about ten o'clock, and remain until mid-night over a fupper nearly of the fame fare as the dinner, and in no lefs abundance.

Such

Such is the life which the richer claffes lead in a country, where there is not even a road, where not a tree is to be feen, the mountains being covered only with heath, where it rains for eight months of the year, and where the fea is in a ftate of perpetual convulfion.

The winter is cold only about two months in the Hebrides, and the fnow lies but a very little time on the ground, but, as tempefts and rains prevail during the greater part of the year, neither wheat nor rye can be brought to perfection in them. Barley and oats, however, thrive here, and are reaped in the month of October, though it is neceffary to dry the grain in kilns to prevent it from fhooting, and to prepare it for being ground.

The greateft part of the barley is fermented and diftilled, to procure a fpirituous liquor which forms their choice delight. It is called whiskey. Oatmeal is made into cakes for bread.

The ifle of Mull is not much more than from twenty to twenty-two miles long, and fifteen or fixteen broad; a mile is termed in the Hebrides *fcoc*. There is nothing like a regular village in the whole ifland; the houfes being

being almoft always fcattered apart, both on the coaft and in the interior. They are conftructed of irregular blocks of bafaltes ranged, without great attention to order, in walls of great thicknefs; for materials of this kind are very plentiful, and always within reach of the builders. The height of the walls fcarcely exceeds five feet, and that of the entrance is feldom above three feet. The more wealthy iflanders, adapt a door to it; but the greater part of the inhabitants are fatisfied to do without any. The roof is often covered with thin pieces of ftone, which is again laid over with turfs. But thofe who can procure a fufficiency of wood for laths ufe a thatch of heath or oaten ftraw, faftened and kept down by long ropes of heath to protect it from the impetuofity of the winds.

The fire-place is always in the middle of the hut, and the fmoke efcapes by a hole in the roof, which is a little to one fide, that the rain may not extinguifh the fire. The Efquimaux and Laplanders difplay much more art and induftry in providing themfelves with habitations.

The iflanders of Mull go both bare-footed and bare-headed, without any regard to rain

or

or froft. The father of a family may sometimes have a Scottish bonnet, and the married women a head-drefs of coarfe linen. But all the young folks, both girls and boys, go about with their heads bare, and without fhoes or ftockings. It fhould be remembered that I am fpeaking of the common clafs of people.

Almoft all are fhepherds or fifhers. Each family has a fmall fpot on which they raife fome barley, oats, and potatoes; which latter, with milk, forms their principal aliment. Thofe on the fea coaft, or by the fide of lakes, fupply themfelves with fifh. They catch falmon, which they dry in the fmoak, and herrings, which they fell, and fometimes make into oil for their lamps.

Thofe who are better informed, or of a more adventurous fpirit, enter into the Englifh navy, and form robuft, fober failors, familiarly acquainted with all the dangers of the fea.

The population of the ifland is about feven thoufand.

It contains three parifhes, nine regular built ftone houfes, and five fchools; its inhabitants profefs the Prefbyterian religion.

The

The women, in general, are fmall, ugly, and ill made; the natural confequence of toil, bad food, the want of fuitable clothing, and the inclemency of the climate. I faw two or three who were a little better looked, and whofe figure was even fomewhat agreeable, but thefe belonged to families in a more comfortable condition. The fun being almoft always covered with clouds, or enveloped in mifts, their skin would be very white, were it not difcoloured by the peat-fmoke, which, from the want of chimnies, continually fills their huts.

Notwithftanding the wetnefs of the climate, I could never perceive that the cuftom of going bare-headed was injurious to the teeth. Both men and women have very fine fets, and are in general, efpecially the men, very healthy. The diforders which might be expected to arife from the frequent rains of this climate, are mitigated by the extreme temperance of their life, exercife, and the purity of the air. Their only fuftenance confifts of milk, potatoes, fifh at certain times of the year, and oatmeal made into a *bouillie* or cakes. Their beverage is pure water; and a few glafsful's of whiskey on
their

their feſtive days conſtitutes their ſupreme happineſs.

On enquiring reſpecting the age of their oldeſt men, Mr. M'Lean of Torloisk aſſured me, that a man of his acquaintance who reſided in the neighbourhood of Aros, had died about ſeven years before at the advanced age of one hundred and ſixteen years, and that there were ſeveral living above eighty; among thoſe, however, it ſhould be remarked, who were in commodious circumſtances.

The horſes of the iſland are of a very diminitive race; its black cattle are equally ſmall, but very delicate when fattened; they are generally exported to England, and they form one of the principal revenues of the iſle of Mull. There are alſo in it two kinds of ſheep which I ſhall ſoon deſcribe, and a few goats; but there are no hogs, and only a few fowls, owing to the difficulty of feeding them. At Aros, in a houſe by the waterſide, I ſaw ſome geeſe and ducks, and three turkies; but the heads of the latter were pale, and I doubt whether they will thrive there.

The

The higheft mountains produce deer, though few in numb r, and of a fmaller fize than the common kind. Heath-cock, of the greater and leffer-fpecies, are very plentiful; there are alfo fome wood-cocks, but no hares. The only fmall bird which I faw in my courfe through it was, the ortolan.

The ifland is now denuded of trees, though formerly it muft have been covered with them. This may be eafily feen by the turberies; on digging which to a certain depth, it rarely happens that roots and ftumps of beech, pine, and birch are not met with. It is my opinion that were the proprietors to give themfelves the trouble of planting evergreens and birches, they would ftill thrive there. In this opinion I am confirmed from a fmall thicket which I faw at *Achnacregs*, on the extremity of the ifle oppofite to that of Torloifk.

The level country and the mountains are in general covered with heath and fod.

The tides rife to a great height in this part, and the fhores abound with fea wreck, which has for fome time back been burnt for its alkali, which fome of the merchants of Glafgow come to purchafe. But this ufeful object

object of induftry is exclufively engroffed by the *lairds*, or a few wealthy perfons. The fea wreck, when frefh, is ufed with fuccefs as a manure.

There are yearly exported from Mull about fifteen hundred head of black cattle; but, from their fmall fize, they bring only about three pounds fterling each.

OF THE SHEEP OF SCOTLAND, PARTICULARLY THOSE OF THE ISLE OF MULL.

I fhall here give an account, in as few words as poffible, of the information which the beft local opportunities enabled me to procure upon this fubject, with the intention of being ufeful to thofe, who occupy themfelves with this great branch of national economy.

In the mountains of Scotland, and the Hebrides, there are only two kinds of fheep; the original race of the country, and a kind which has been introduced from England, and which is accordingly called *Englifh fheep*.

The wool of the former, or Scottifh fheep, is much fuperior to that of the Englifh fheep, and even approaches the Spanifh wool in finenefs ness. But many people prefer the English kind becaufe they yield a fleece double that of the Scottish race, are fatter and fuller of flesh. They accordingly fell at a much higher price.

An English sheep, in good condition, fells upon the spot, for half a guinea and often twelve shillings; whilst a Scottish one feldom brings above six or seven shillings.

The wool is fold here by a weight of twenty-four pounds, denominated a stone; this quantity is generally valued at from six to seven shillings. The pound contains sixteen ounces.

The flocks of sheep range the mountains or valleys, both night and day, summer and winter, without any shelter; yet the extreme wetness of the climate does not feem to do them the leaft injury.

They never have any fodder during the winter, not even when there is snow; but it should be observed, that, in thefe ifles, though in fo northern a latitude, the snow does not continue long on the ground. By a very rare occurrence, in the winter of 1783, it remained upon it about two months; during which time, the sheep fed upon the tops of a tall kind of broom which remained above the fnow. The poor animals, however, fuffered feverely during that winter, and became very meagre. But a much greater number of them died from accident, than from want or difeafe ; and on the reappearance of the grafs they recruited very faft, and fattened as ufual.

The rams are carefully feparated from the ewes in the month of September, and are not admitted among them again till the twentieth of November, that the lambs may be yeaned only in the beft feafon.

The ewe brings forth and takes care of her lamb without any affiftance. The fhepherd, who, from time to time, vifits his numerous flocks, to prevent them from ftraying too far, or endangering themfelves amidft the rocky precipices, takes the number of the young lambs, who foon run after their dams and crop the new fprung herb.

In the third month after parturition the lambs are taken away from their mothers, being then ftrong enough to do without them, and are formed into flocks which are put into feparate enclofures, under the care of a keeper.

When

When the pasture grounds are contiguous and of great extent, one man and two dogs are sufficient to keep fifteen hundred sheep. But when the pastures are of inconsiderable extent, and it is necessary that they should feed more regularly, a keeper and two dogs are requisite for every eight hundred.

Nineteen or twenty rams are sufficient for eight hundred ewes. The keeper repairs every evening to a cottage in the form of a dwelling-house, erected in the midst of the pasture ground.

The only disorders to which the sheep are subject here, are the pleurisy, which happens but seldom, and the staggers, which turns their heads to one side, and always ends in their death. This disease is unfortunately very frequent, and often attacks those which appear to be the most healthy *.

The

* This disease is the same as that known in Tuscany by the name of *Pazzia*. The animals affected with it, and which are called in France *moutons lourds, moutons imbécilles*, waddle in their walk. Abbé Fontana, in a letter upon this subject addressed to M. Darcet, and inserted in the *Journal de physique*, tom. i. page 227, 1784, says, " it is " very remarkable that the sheep attacked by it, generally " fall on one side, and that the vesicle, which occasions it " is found to be in the lobe of the brain opposite to the " side on which they fall. This observation holds good
" in

The Hebridians never give any falt to their sheep; they are not however ignorant of its good effect; but their flocks being very numerous, and the falt, from government duties and carriage, extremely dear, the expence would be too great for their abilities. Were it not for this hindrance, the inhabitants would undoubtedly ufe it for the fleecy race; for they are very fenfible that the cows and oxen, who feed upon the herbs wafhed by the fea, thrive well, become plump, and have a fleek fkin.

Here I ought to mention a cuftom ufed in feveral parts of the north of Scotland, particularly in the lower diftricts, though it is not practifed in the Hebrides or more inland parts of the Highlands, I mean that of fmearing their fheep with tar.

" in all cafes; and the animals conftantly fall on the fame
" fide." The celebrated phyfician of Tufcany, from feveral
microfcopic experiments on the liquor contained in thefe
veficles or *idatides* in the brain of fheep, concludes, that
" the particles, which are feen floating in that liquor, are
" *real animalcules.*" This new and fingular difcovery,
fays that learned philofopber, " may throw light on fome
" diforders of the human brain, and even on infanity; fince
" veficles as large as a pea, and fometimes larger, have been
" found in the brains of perfons who have died of that ma-
" lady, which is fo terrible and humiliating to human va-
" nity," page 231 of the fame paper.

The owners of the numerous flocks of thefe diftricts, where the winter is far feverer than in the Hebrides, entertain an opinion that the intenfe cold makes the fheep fcabby ; and as a fecurity againft this, they make ufe of the following prefervative :

In the month of November each fhepherd takes two barrels of tar and one barrel of butter; or a greater quantity of each, according to the number of the flock, but always in the proportion of two-thirds of tar to one-third of butter. Thefe two fubftances are then boiled or melted together; and after being completely mixed and permitted to cool, each fheep is tied up by the feet, ftretched on a hurdle, and rubbed over with the compofition. This operation is performed by feparating the wool into thin flakes that the tar may be applied to the skin with as little injury as poffible to the fleece.

According to the opinion of the fheepfarmers of the country, two advantages refult from this practice. The firft is, the preferving of the cattle in a ftate of health; the fecond, that of making them yield a greater quantity

quantity of wool. The moſt wealthy ſheep-farmers, whom I had an opportunity of conſulting upon the ſubject, aſſured me, that the fleece was certainly more abundant when the ſheep were tarred; but they, at the ſame time ſtated, that it ſells for nearly one-half leſs than unſmeared wool, being rendered a great deal heavier than its real weight, by the dirt which adheres to the tar. The operation by which the tar may be taken off, conſiſts in ſoaking the fleece after it is ſhorn in warm-water, into which butter has been melted. But this proceſs muſt be expenſive; and the wool never reaches the quality of its natural ſtate.

Five thouſand ſheep require twenty barrels of tar, and one-third that quantity of butter. This expence appears at firſt much more conſiderable than it really is; for, on dividing it among five thouſand, it does not amount to five *ſols* a-head. Beſides, this compoſition of butter and tar gives the ſheep a ſort of artificial fat, which ſupplies what the rigour of the climate deprives them of; and if it tends to keep theſe uſeful animals in better health, and alſo to encreaſe the quantity

tity of their wool, however ridiculous, expensive or difficult to those unaccustomed to it, the practice may at first appear, it is yet, perhaps, worthy of profound attention and examination on the part of those who are particularly interested in this important branch of economy.

CHAPTER VI.

Departure from Torloisk.—Stay at Aros.—Visit to two worthy Farmers and Brothers, the Stuarts of Aros.—Excursion to the Mountain of Benmore, the highest in the Isle of Mull.—Stop at Mr. Campbel's, of Knock.—His agricultural Operations.—Curious Lavas.—Departure from Aros for Achnacregs.

I WAS treated with such engaging marks of politeness and affection by Mr. M'Lean and all his family, as well as by his visitors, that it was impossible for me to leave them without feeling a sentiment of gratitude and regret. I should be happy to prove to them that they will never fade from my remembrance. This respectable philosopher kindly accompanied us for several miles on our return.

During my stay at Mr. L'Lean's I took a survey of the volcanic hills in his vicinity, and directed my researches to the right and left of his house, along a tract of coast which the waves have washed into naked precipices
capable

capable of affording a complete view of the structure of substances formerly acted upon by subterraneous fire. I shall give a description of them in the chapter appropriated to the mineralogy of the isle of Mull.

We set off, mounted upon little half-wild horses, and on the same day reached Aros. Here we remained the whole of next day in a very uncomfortable lodging, where we found only some barley meal, which was made into pottage for us with milk, a little smoke-dried salmon, and a few sheep-trotters; no wine nor beer; but whisky, which scalded our mouths, and, to crown all, our beds were of the very worst kind. Our host, however, was a good sort of man, and used every possible exertion for our accommodation. With this we expressed ourselves satisfied for the present; and he promised to procure us some fresh fish by the next morning.

Of these, two of my companions were left to enjoy the benefit, for I had determined myself to set out with the first dawn to visit the high mountain of Benmore, and William Thornton, who now felt an increased ardour for the pursuits of Natural History, resolved to accompany me.

There

There are not much more than three miles from Aros to Knock, along a pretty good road, which here and there prefents fome picturefque landfcapes, of an appearance, however, fomewhat wild.

On a meadow in the bottom of a narrow valley, wafhed by the fea, we obferved one of thofe columns called *Cairns*, of which, from the ground being overflowed at the time, I was unable to procure the dimenfions. But as near as I could judge by the eye, it might be about fourteen or fifteen feet in height, and feemed to confift of grit ftone. There is certainly fomething aftonifhing in the frequency of thefe ancient monuments through the Hebrides and the main land of Scotland. Popular tradition traces every one of them back to the time of Offian, which is merely to fay, that their origin has been loft in the lapfe of ages.

The houfe of Mr. Campbel, of Knock, is very agreeably fituated at the foot of a high mountain, and not far from an arm of the fea, very plentiful in fifh. Mr. Campbel was gone at this time to Oban, but the miftrefs of the houfe received us in the moft affable manner, and treated us with tea and rum.

We

We requested that she would procure us a guide to direct our way to the top of Ben-more; but her son, a youth of seventeen or eighteen years old, offered to accompany us himself. This young man, who had a very agreeable figure, and was dressed in the Hebridian stile, immediately presented us with fowling-pieces, saying, that he had excellent dogs, and that we should certainly find some *black-cocks*; for he had no conception that we could wish to climb so rugged a mountain, for any other purpose than the pleasures of the chace, which he passionately loved himself. He was, therefore, much surprised when I took out my hammers, and told him, that I had come to examine the stones of the place On receiving that information, he shewed us immense heaps of them which had been taken off a considerable tract which his father had cleared in the midst of some lavas. All these stones, broken into small lumps, were afterwards used to form enclosures to a piece of ground which required much labour, time and expence, to reclaim. A larger collection of lavas is seldom met with than this presented. I shall presently mention its particulars.

As

As we intended to return to Aros in the evening, we loft no time in beginning to fcale the fteep fides of Benmore. In my travels among the high Alps I never experienced fo much difficulty as in this afcent. An almoft impenetrable heath, growing upon a marfhy foil, covers the bafis, the middle and the fummit of the mountain, which rifes in the fhape of a fugar loaf. It is impoffible to make any progrefs, but by following the fmall gullies which the waters have worn, and walking in the very midft of the flender ftreams, which occupy the bottom of thefe fteep and narrow paths. The black and bufhy heath fpreads its gloomy veil over thofe ftones, which might intereft and repay the fatigues of the naturalift. Not a fingle plant, nor fo much as a tuft of mofs is to be feen, every thing is here fmothered by its deftructive progrefs.

The ftones which the moft confiderable gullies have uncovered, and thofe which have been broken off by froft, are all volcanic. But they prefent no variety; all of them are whitifh-grey lavas, flightly maculated with zeolite.

We had reached to a confiderable height, when, wearied with feeing only the fame lavas,

lavas, and meeting with no other plant than the toilſome heath, whence ſtarted from time to time ſome black-cocks, which young Campbel brought to the ground with great dexterity, I reſolved to go no farther. But William Thornton braving every difficulty and deſirous to gain the higheſt ſummit, proceeded onward. The ſtones which he brought down with him afforded no variety. Upon the whole, the mountain of Benmore, notwithſtanding its height, and a kind of reſemblance which it has at a diſtance to mount Veſuvius, does not repay the trouble of aſcending it. We gladly returned therefore to reſt ourſelves at Knock, where the lavas being much more intereſting, I made a collection of ſome ſpecimens. We then took leave of young Campbel and his mother, notwithſtanding their preſſing ſolicitations to ſtop, and proceeded for Aros, where we were expected.

It was determined that we ſhould ſet off for Achnacregs at ten next morning. This was a diſtance of eighteen or twenty miles, which we willingly performed by land, as we ſhould thus have an opportunity of examining that part of the iſland, and at the ſame time avoid the navigation of the tempeſtuous ſound of Mull;

for

for from Achnacregs we could next morning eafily reach Oban to breakfaft.

We left Aros at the appointed hour; but firft had the pleafure of breakfafting, by invitation, with the Meffrs. Stuarts of Aros.

Thefe two gentlemen, who are brothers, occupy a commodious habitation on a fmall hill, which they have brought into cultivation, and rendered productive of pafturage, barley, oats, and potatoes. In that modeft afylum, free from care and difturbance, they pafs away their days with a happinefs which ambition has never tafted. Two intelligent and induftrious fifters partake with them in the management of their houfehold affairs. Here they enjoy all the gentle delight of rural life; I fincerely wifh that they only lived under a more favourable fky, and on a foil capable of exercifing their agricultural tafte and talents to more advantage.

We took leave of them at ten in the morning of the 29th of November.

A few miles from Aros, near the waterfide, we obferved the ruins of a catholic chapel, where are ftill vifible a gothic baffo-relievo in freeftone, reprefenting the Virgin Mary between two feraphims, and a large grave-

grave-ftone which exhibits the effigy of a warrior in complete armour, that is, with helmet, bracelet, cuifhes, buckler, and fword. One of our guides told us, that it was the figure of a hero of the clan of M'Lean. Befide this fepulchral relic, we obferved another reprefenting alfo in relievo, a woman of tall ftature, dreffed in the gothic ftyle of the ancient ladies of France. The name of the place where we difcovered thefe ruins is *Galchayle.*

Thence we continued our courfe along a way, which might be called rather a path than a road, to *Lenigorn, Ardmitrail,* and *Corinahinifh.* It muft not be fuppofed that all thefe names indicate villages, or even hamlets. Alas! they are applied only to fome huts, fcattered at diftant intervals amidft thefe difmal deferts.

Every thing along this road is volcanic; but the compact homogeneous grey-coloured lavas which it prefents, are not very interefting. They are befides fo thickly covered with mofs or lichens, that it is neceffary to break them before they can be diftinguifhed.

In the vicinity of *Ledkirk,* however, I found fome hard compact lava, difpofed in
                                                      flabs,

flabs, which gave me confiderable pleafure. This lava was of a white kind; and at firft fight might be taken for a fine limeftone of that colour. But on a more attentive examination, its vitreous appearance proves beyond doubt that it is merely a bafaltic lava bleached by its contiguity to fome crater, or by remaining long in a fluid impregnated with fome acid. It is remarkable that thefe lavas have preferved their magnetic property. I collected fome fpecimens to compare them with fome of the fame kind which I found on Mount Mezinc, in Vivarais, and to thofe of the extinct volcanos in the environs of Padua, and of the Euganean mountains.

From Ledkirk we paffed on to *Garmony*, and thence to *Scallafdel*, leaving the little fort of Duard on our left. On a green rifing ground, near Scallafdel, we faw a druidical circle, formed of very large pieces of rough granite. We ftopped for a moment to examine this altar or temple; but quitted it haftily and with indignation, on reflecting that here the cruel priefts, of a ftill more cruel religion, had, perhaps, facrificed fome Iphigenia, thrown by a tempeft upon this new Taurica.

We

We arrived in the evening at Achnacregs. This is the name of a small creek, where there is only one house, wretched and smoky, of two stories however, and with chimnies. From its first appearance, it was difficult to know whether it was a farm-house or an inn; we found that it was both the one and the other. The arm of the sea which separates this part of the isle of Mull from Oban, the opposite point of the main land of Scotland, being of inconsiderable breadth, the passage is much frequented for the transportation of cattle; and this house affords shelter to those who are driven in by bad weather, or who come to the island on commercial pursuits. Our entertainment here was in the style of Hebridian frugality; but, our landlord was a good sort of man, very inquisitive after news, somewhat of an antiquary, and had as much veneration for Fingal and Ossian, as the Jews have for Moses.

A heavy rain detained us within doors the whole of next day; I employed the time, therefore, in ticketing my specimens, and arranging my journal.

On the succeeding day, the rain was not so thick and frequent, but the sea was very boisterous. We made some excursions in the vicinity; and about half a mile from our lodging obferved a bank of lime-ftone adjoining a bed of free-ftone, and both of them inclofed in a current of lava.

At a fhort diftance from this bank, we came to a large rough column of freeftone, lying flat on the ground, and broken in the middle. On meafuring, I found it to be twenty-one feet long. Our hoft, who accompanied us at this time, did not fail to excite our admiration of this ancient monument. " Never was there a perfon, except " Offian," faid he, " who could move this enor- " mous ftone. The operation of time, or per- " haps an earthquake has overthrown it, and " now there is not one in the ifland who can " fet it up again."

It rained all the morning of the following day; but towards the evening it became fair for a little. Count Andreani, who began to be weary of fo difmal a folitude, and fo bad a lodging, refolved to take advantage of this fhort interval, to crofs over to Oban, where he fhould wait our arrival. The only veffel which the place afforded, was a fmall fkiff, very badly equipped, and rowed by two boys, of whom the eldeft was not more than fourteen years. The wind was variable, and the

the fea not very fmooth. In vain, however, did I reprefent to him that it were better to wait till the next morning; nothing could prevail on him to ftop. He fet off in the fkiff, with his two fervants, at half paft four, telling us, that he fhould fleep in a good bed, and eat a better fupper than we, at the houfe of the brothers Stevenfons, of Oban, where he expected to arrive by feven the fame evening.

Lefs adventurous, though perhaps more prudent, than Andreani, I perfuaded William Thornton to remain with me at Achnacregs, till the fea became more moderate. After wifhing our friend a good paffage, and looking after him as far as we could fee him, we flowly returned to our wretched and dreary habitation. I wrote till eight; we then fupped, and I went to bed at ten.

The wind by this time increafed to a violent gale, accompanied with a great deal of rain; but I was nowife anxious refpecting the fituation of my companion, whom I imagined fafe in Oban long before.

I had fcarcely fhut my eyes, however, when a loud noife awaked me. I heard a rapping and calling at the door; I rofe, and after informing the people of the houfe, who went and opened it, we faw our poor friend Andreani

dreani enter with his attendants, as completely drenched, as if they had been repeatedly plunged under water. They were overtaken by a ſtorm, when half way over, and though ſeveral times driven near to Oban, they were unable to make the harbour. The night was ſo dark, that it was almoſt impoſſible to know where they were, and it was not without encountering the greateſt dangers, and in a manner by mere chance, that they regained the little haven of Achnacregs.

They were numbed with cold; our firſt care, therefore, was to warm them. A large fire was lighted, rum and tea were given them to drink, and every poſſible means were taken to recover them. Count Andreani was himſelf the firſt to laugh at his adventure; but his two ſervants, who had never before travelled beyond the fertile and ſmiling fields of Italy, and who, therefore, felt ſomewhat aukward in their preſent ſituation, were not ſo merrily diſpoſed. They were ſo deeply impreſſed with the dangers and frightful appearance of a ſtormy ſea, amidſt the darkneſs of night, that, returning a thouſand thanks to the Bleſſed Virgin, who had heard their invocation and brought them ſafe to land, they raiſed their hands to heaven, and ſwore, that they

they would never again leave the ifland, barren as it was. "We fhould prefer," faid they, "to crop the herbs in this place, to expofing ourfelves, a fecond time, to the fury of that abominable fea." They then muttered their difpleafure at their mafter's mprudence and folly, in coming to vifit the noft deteftable country in the world. Their pantomimic geftures, the expreffion of their countenances, and the ferious tone of their amentations, entertained me with a fcene truly comic.

Repofe during the remaining part of the night, and the appearance of a fine morning, partly effaced the impreffions of the preceding evening. The fea, however, was not yet navigable; and the beft means of diffipating tedium was to betake myfelf to active employment.

At fun-rife, therefore, I made one of thofe excurfions from which there is always derived fome benefit, either for inftruction or health, and in which I always find my advantage, in whatever country I may travel.

A vaft black rock, perfectly perpendicular, and almoft infulated, forced itfelf upon my attention, ever fince my arrival at Achnacregs.

cregs. I conjectured that it might be a bafaltic colonade, and I wifhed to afcertain the truth of this conjecture. After walking about a mile and a quarter, I arrived at the foot of one of the moft aftonifhing productions of volcanic combuftion that I ever had an opportunity of obferving.

It prefented the appearance of an ancient circus, formed of natural walls of bafaltes, rifing perpendicularly with fo regular a conftruction, that at firft view, the fpectator cannot avoid thinking it to be the production of human induftry and art. But the utmoft ftretch of human force, heightened by all the aid of the mechanic powers, could never have been capable of elevating fuch enormous maffes. The whole muft be regarded as the effect of a vaft combuftion, which, inftead of deftroying, has here produced appearances analogous to thofe of a creative power.

This grand natural monument excited a juft admiration and even enthufiafm in my mind. I fpent two hours in viewing, ftudying, and obferving it over again in different points of view, and I was ftill unwearied of gazing upon it. I went in queft of my companions, who were tranfported with no lefs admiration than myfelf at the fight of thefe vaft

bafaltic

bafaltic walls, ftanding alone, and rifing in a bold and perpendicular fabrick around a circular fpace, which prefented an arena that would have been well adapted to the games of the ancients.

It is no lefs remarkable, that the acceffory parts of this fingular production of fubterraneous fire feem to have been placed in the vicinity, as if with the defign of furnifhing a key to the problem of its formation.

I meafured, with the moft fcrupulous attention, the height and thicknefs of the walls, and the diameter of the circular enclofure.

On the 6th day, I vifited it once more. In the afternoon of that day, the weather beginning to affume a more fettled appearance, Count Andreani faid, that he was refolved to try his fortune a fecond time, and that he fhould fet off at four o'clock; which he accordingly did. The wind was at this time favourable, and as the fkiff could not carry us all, we fuffered him to proceed, promifing, that we fhould fpeedily follow him.

He fent back the boat, during the night, with a fupply of eatables, for our cheer had been but very poor and fcanty for fome days before, having exhaufted almoft the whole ftock of Achnacregs.

This supply was extremely useful, as the storm returned by the next morning, and the sea ran too high for us to trust ourselves upon it in so frail a vehicle. I employed the time in new excursions, and in arranging my notes, particularly those which related to the mineralogical history of the isle of Mull. These I have thrown into a separate section, that such of my readers as are interested in that science may find the objects which refer to it, united under one head, and that those to whom the subject may be indifferent or tiresome, may easily pass it over. It may not be improper to mention a second time, that this is my ordinary mode of proceeding.

At length, on the evening of the 6th of October, which was the eighth of our confinement, a bark having come in to Achnacregs with a cargo of beeves, which was to return on the morrow, we resolved to embrace the opportunity of a passage in her; we accordingly embarked at six next morning, not for Oban, but for the isle of Kerrera, where we landed at eight. We walked along the isle, which is very small, and at its extremity found a boat, which conveyed us in less than one hour to Oban, where our friend Andreani most impatiently expected our arrival.

CHAP-

CHAPTER VII.

Natural History of the Island of Mull.

THIS island, which is one of the largest of the Hebrides, is not more than from twenty to twenty-two miles in length, and fifteen or sixteen in breadth; but being of a very irregular form, it may be stated at eighty miles in circumference at least.

I shall proceed to describe the parts which I visited, in the order of my journey. Those who would wish to explore the island in the same pursuit, by disembarking at Achnacregs, coming back to Aros, and travelling along the left bank of the sound of Mull, will trace my itinerary by commencing where I finished it.

AROS.

A R O S.

ROAD FROM AROS TO TORLOISK.

Columns of Bafaltes. Lavas, compact, black, grey, reddish, intermixed with Globules of white Zeolite. Blocks of rounded Granite on the Summit of some bafaltic Mountains.

THE ancient caftle of Aros, once the refidence of the famous M'Donald of the Ifles, now prefents nothing more than a ruin. Its remains ftand on a fmall colonade of bafaltes by the brink of the fea, and on the right fide of the entrance of the fmall bay of Aros.

The river of Aros, which might with more propriety be called as a pretty large brook, takes its rife from a marfhy tract, about the middle of the ifland. From its fource to its mouth it runs on a compact lava, which varies in colour from a deep black to grey and reddifh. This lava is in general durable and compact; fome beds of it, however, are found of a gravelly and friable texture.

Thefe compact lavas contain, in general, fo great a quantity of knobs of white zeolite, that this laft matter may be faid to form nearly one-third of the weight of the lava.

The zeolite is found here in a globular form, and in general about the bignefs of a

pea.

pea. Some of the globules are radiated; but they are more frequently cryftalized in a confufed manner, and without any determinate form. I found nothing of this kind fufficiently interefting for the cabinet of the naturalift, from Aros to Torloisk. The reafon, was obvious. Every thing was fo covered with mofs, lichens and heath, that I was forced to confine my refearches to the bed of the fmall river, and to fome gullies connected with it, where the rock was fomewhat expofed.

As we drew near to Torloisk, at the diftance of about three miles from the caftle, we came to fome mountains entirely volcanic, and at leaft two hundred and fifty toifes high. It excited my aftonifhment as I paffed along their fummit to obferve fome large blocks of granite, rolled and partly rounded, detached from each other, and refting on the volcanic matter, to which, however, they do not adhere, having been evidently tranfported hither by the effect of fome convulfion. For adventitious bodies of that kind, and of fo great bulk, found on mountains and in an ifland where there is no folid rock of granite, muft have been depofited here by fome very powerful revolution.

Thefe

These lumps of granite may have been ejected from granitic quarries, which perhaps existed at great depths under these ancient volcanos, by the explosions which took place at the epoch when extensive combustions devastated these countries, and formed groups of islands which appear to have the same origin.

It is besides within the verge of possibility, that those parts of the mountains where they are now found, were not at that period elevated summits, but rather formed part of the bottom of the sea; and that these granitic blocks were rolled from a distance by the currents. It is possible, that circumstances of subterraneous explosion, equally terrible with those which formed the isle of Santorini, in the Archipelago, or Montenove, in Italy, may have raised up the bottom of the sea into volcanic peaks; or, if it should appear more plausible to some, we may refer to a period when mountains still higher were entirely covered with the sea; a fact, which cannot be doubted, since marine bodies are found in great abundance in beds of lime-stone or clay, situated on the Alps or Apennines, at a height three or four times greater. But the subject would require illustrations, which the nature of this work does not permit me to enter into.

TOR-

TORLOISK.

Black Bafaltes, with and without Zeolite; altered Lava, which has loft its Hardnefs and its Colour; Bafaltes calcined on the Surface of a Blood-red Colour, and having the Appearance of a clayey Bole.

At a little diftance from Mr. M'Lean's houfe, near the road leading to the fea on the fide of Kilnynen, is an extent of rugged fteep rocks bounding the coaft, which are beat upon by the waves and by frequent rains. They are eafily obferved along the whole of that part of the coaft, being entirely bare.

This craggy tract which extends as far as *Loch-mari*, is compofed of different currents of bafaltic lava, of a deep black colour. Several of thefe ftreams are formed of irregular maffes, others of tables, and fome have affumed a prifmatic form. Here I found fome pretty large fpecimens of fine zeolite, feveral of which were cryftallized into cubes, fome had the appearance of diverging rays, and others were a little calcedonious. They are in general very white, but there are fome

which

which have become fallow from the decompofition of their iron, and feveral alfo have a a light greenifh tint. They are moft frequently feen in large lumps buried in the lava; but thofe which have adopted the cubical form, are often found in the fiffures which feparate the different ftreams of lava.

The traveller fhould not omit vifiting on the oppofite quarter, that is, towards the path on his left as he proceeds from Mr. M'Lean's houfe to the fhore, a quarry, out of which all the ftones of his buildings have been taken. Here there are found feveral lavas which are worthy of attention. They may be obferved with the fame facility as the preceding; the interior of the volcanic eminence being completely expofed to view by digging away the ftones.

The upper beds of the quarry are formed of a black hard compact lava, containing fome globules of white zeolite.

Thofe immediately below, having been probably acted upon by the fulphurous acid, have loft a part of their colour and their hardnefs. They are grey, whitifh, and moft frequently of the colour of iron ruft. The zeolite which is found buried in it, has preferved

its

its forms and chymical properties, but has notwithstanding assumed various tints.

Other beds, still lower, have sustained a more considerable and different kind of alteration; they are of a bright red, and contain, as well as the lavas over them, some globules of zeolite, unaltered with respect to their principles, but softer and a little coloured. The lava itself has lost its hardness.

The lavas of this quarry, though of the same texture and composition, have undergone different modifications, as well from the exhalations which rise from this burnt soil, as from the action and effects of long continued fire.

The different craters afford a constant and remarkable example of the active operation of the vapours, not only on the colours, but also on the grain and hardness of the lavas which they decompose, and form into new combinations of gypsum, iron, allum, sulphur, &c. I have proofs, likewise, that the long continued application of fire, will, in certain circumstances, transform the hardest and blackest lavas, basaltes for example, into a state of red calx, if I may use that expression.

These

Thefe fuperficially calcined lavas in lofing their firft colour, lofe alfo the elements of their hardnefs; and there are circumftances in which they become foft and foapy to the touch like fat clays. I have defcribed a variety of this kind in my *Mineralogy of Volcanos*, page 395, No. 10.

It is, therefore, of effential importance to diftinguifh accurately the two kinds of alteration which I have mentioned, and of which the one is owing to the action of acids, and the other to that of long applied heat. Thus the black lavas which compofe the firft beds of the volcanic quarry of Torloisk are nowife altered. Thofe which fucceed them, and which are grey and whitifh, feem to have been difcoloured and altered by acid vapours; whilft the deepeft ftrata, in which the lava is of a blood-red colour and friable texture, appear to derive that modification folely from the long continued action of fire, and a real calcination of the furface. In this cafe the fire has not been fufficiently violent to change the lava into a vitreous fubftance; but its prolonged operation has difunited its parts, and rufted and oxidified its ferruginous particles, which have changed to a red colour, like that of the calx of lead, which a very violent

violent and long applied heat, converts into the moſt beautiful minium. The globular zeolite which is found in the upper as well lower ſtrata of the quarry of Torloisk, that is, in the black, grey or whitiſh lavas, is the ſame. It is the ſame alſo in the deepeſt beds, where the lava is more altered and has become red. This zeolite differs from that of the other beds only in being a little ſofter; but the difference is not very perceptible.

What has happened here as to the zeolites, has taken place alſo with reſpect to pointed ſchorl in a lava of *Chenavari* in Vivarais. The black ſchorl remains almoſt untouched in the midſt of a lava altered and turned to a red colour by the continued action of a ſtrong fire, but which has not been able to vitrify it*.

I have

---

* The following is the paſſage of the *Mineralogy of Volcanos*:—" Argillaceous baſaltes of a blood red, with ſpecks
" of black ſchorl in the moſt excellent preſervation,
" though the lava itſelf is changed completely into an
" argillaceous matter ſoft and ſoapy."—*Mineralogy of Volcanos*, page 395, No. 10, in 8vo. Paris, 1784.

I ought to add here, that in ſaying, that the lava had changed into an argillaceous matter, I did not mean that it had paſſed into the ſtate of real clay. My intention was merely

I have quoted in the same work, which I published in 1784, on the Mineralogy of Volcanos, a daily example of this superficial calcination effected by art. In Vivarais, and also on the other bank of the Rhone, lime-kilns are constructed with their interior lining of very black and hard basaltic lava. The pit-coal fewel, with which these kilns are continually supplied, soon vitrifies the whole of the inner surface, which then runs into one piece. But as the vitrification does not penetrate above four or five lines in the blocks of lava, which are several feet thick, the part in immediate contact with it, being exposed to a less degree of heat, passes at length into a state of calcination. Its colour becomes red, its hardness is destroyed, and when the

---

merely to state that the lava thus altered had put on the exterior appearance of clays; that is, that it was tender, earthy, and soft to the touch. I am the more desirous to explain myself upon this subject, because several naturalists, who have written upon volcanos, have taken these substances for real clays, regarding them not merely as earthified lavas, but as embodied clays burnt by subterraneous fires. In these cases, however, the schorls, cryolites, zeolites, and even pieces of porous lava which are found in it, remove every doubt respecting the identity of these altered lavas with those which join or cover them, or lie in alternate order with others, and which are perfectly found.

kilns

kilns are taken down or repaired, it is eafy to obferve through the thicknefs of the lava, the gradual action exerted by a heat fo violent and long continued. The reader will excufe this digreffion, which is by no means foreign to the fubject.

KNOCK.

MOUNTAIN OF BENMORE, THREE MILES FROM AROS.

Lavas in Slabs, prifms, and irregular Maffes, hard, found, compact; internally of a blackifh grey, externally of a dull white; decompofed to the Depth of four or five Lines, and exhibiting the primitive Elements of their Compofition; in fome of them are found Globules and Dots of white Zeolite.

In mentioning the mountain of Benmore, I faid that it was covered with heath fo thick as hardly to permit me to difcover the lava of which it is compofed. But on paffing through feveral hollows formed by the water which runs down its fides, I obferved only one kind of lava, which is grey, hard, compact, and inter-

intermixed with feveral globules of zeolite. I carefully examined feveral of thefe chafms from the bottom to the top of the mountain, and no where did I meet with any other kind of lava. But, as the way was very difficult, I was able to vifit the north fide only of this volcanic peak. I therefore invite thofe naturalifts who may follow me in the fame journey, to attempt the fouth fide of the mountain, to difcover whether the lavas there be equally homogeneous.

Knock is the name of the refidence of Mr. Campbel; and to diftinguifh him from other perfons of the fame clan, he is defcribed by the appellation of Campbel of Knock.

His houfe, fituated on an eminence, at the foot of Benmore, has a view on one fide of a delightful valley, covered with flocks, and, on the other, of a fine loch or arm of the fea, navigable, rich in fifh, and vifited by the herring at the time of their migration.

A confiderable tract which he has cleared in the midft of the lavas, to obtain the fmall quantity of foil produced by their decompofition, muft have required a labour which nothing but the moft inflexible conftancy, fupported by the hope of fertilizing and embellifhing

bellifhing the place of his habitation, could have been capable of furmounting.

This vaft undertaking produced confiderable quantities of volcanic ftones, broken, fplit, and cut in various directions; from which the ground is cleared by forming them into dry walls of great extent and proportionate thicknefs. Thefe enclofures, which are very numerous, prefent to the naturalift a moft agreeable field of obfervation. The lavas are compact, and of a black or rather deep grey colour approaching black. They are frequently difpofed in tables, fometimes in prifms, and at other times in irregular maffes. Their fracture prefents a pafte of a homogeneous appearance, of a grain compact, fmooth and fufceptible, of a fine polifh. But a peculiar alteration obfervable on its furface, and which has penetrated a few lines into its interior, merits all the attention of the naturalift, and renders this kind of lavas very interefting.

This alteration, operated by time, or rather by the different modifications of the air upon the lavas, has difcovered their conftituent principles. It may be regarded as a fort of natural diffection, which, by deftroying certain parts, has expofed to view thofe which would otherwife remain concealed, and which no chymical analyfis could have ever brought to light. This requires a more particular explanation; which I proceed to give, with a fpecimen in my hand, that thofe who may have occafion to obferve fimilar lavas, which are very common in the ancient extinct volcanos of France, may be better able to correct my errors, if they fháll be of opinion that I have committed any, or make ufe with me of a means which may fometimes difcover to what ftone a particular lava belonged before its fufion.

The lavas in queftion I repeat, appear on being broken, of a hard compact texture, and of a dark grey colour, approaching to black. The particles feem well amalgamated and homogeneous; nor does the microfcope even difcover any difference between them.

If we proceed to the examination of their exterior parts, we find their furface grained, unequal, and rugged to the touch, and exhibiting cryftals and plates of felt fpar, jutting points of black fchorl, fixed often in the felt fpar itfelf, and both the one and the other furrounded with fmall cavities, by which
they

they are completely infulated, and which prove that the particles, amidſt which the felt ſpar and ſchorl were incloſed, have been deſtroyed.

The white cryſtals of felt ſpar are ſlightly touched with a reddiſh tint; which is a little deeper in the interſtices where it has been more difficult for the rain-water to inſinuate itſelf, and to waſh away the ochreous particles produced by the decompoſition of iron.

The naturaliſt, moſt experienced in lithology, on ſeeing their decompoſed ſurface, cannot avoid regarding them, at firſt view, as real granites. He does not find himſelf embarraſſed, until he examines their fracture and their interior texture, and eſpecially until he preſents to the magnet the unaltered part which attracts it as ſtrongly as baſaltic lava of the richeſt iron ore; whilſt the exterior cruſt has no impreſſion upon it.

It thence reſults, that the iron which forms one of the conſtituent principles of this lava, has ſuſtained a complete change of its natural properties, in which it has been accompanied with the earthy particles which were combined or united with it.

This connexion being deftroyed, the fubftances which efcaped decompofition, fuch as felt fpar, fchorl, and feveral fmall pieces of quartz have been exhibited to view; fo that on removing the covering under which they are concealed, it is not very difficult to difcover their organization.

Their original ftate appears, therefore, to have been that of a granitic or porphyric rock. The naturalift will more ready decide in favour of the latter. from the confideration that the bafis of real porphyric is in general petrofilex, which, whatever be its hardnefs or its colour, is fometimes found decompofed naturally in the open air, and is alfo capable of being acted upon by fulphurous acid vapours.

But to be affured that this lava owes its exiftence to a porphyric fubftance, with a bafis of petrofilex, nothing elfe is required than to fufe with the blow-pipe a fmall fragment of the foundeft part, that is, the part which has preferved its hardnefs and its black colour, and the refult will foon appear to be a white enamel, which is a characteriftic mark of petrofilices; whereas the lava with a horn-ftone bafis produces a fine enamel of a

deep

deep black colour. My learned friend, Deodat Dolomieu, has sufficiently established that distinction in his excellent memoirs.

Similar lavas are found at the foot of Mount Mezinc, in the Vivarais, near Pui, in Velai, on the Euganean mountains, and in the isles of Ponces.

It always presents itself as a subject of astonishment, on examining certain lavas, that subterraneous fires should have melted into a stream, stones which now appear of the hardest consistence, and that with scarcely any change in their primitive organization.

LEDIRKILL.

ROAD FROM AROS TO ACHNACREGS.

White compact Lavas which have preserved their hardness.

On the road to Ledirkill, I observed some hard compact and very white lavas. They do not appear to have undergone any alteration, either spontaneously, or by means of emanations of gas. Their texture is pretty homogeneous; but the particles are a little scaly,

scaly, and bear a resemblance to those of a certain felt spar.

Their white colour does not seem to announce the presence of iron. But one would be led into an error by trusting to their first appearance; for they have a very sensible action on the loadstone. There are some white mines of very rich spathose iron, of which the colour does not exhibit the least indication.

The white lavas of Ledirkill have some resemblance to stones of tolfa with this difference, that the latter are nowise magnetic, and that the former produce no allum.

I am therefore induced to consider the lavas of Ledirkill, as naturally white, and as deriving their existence from stones of the same nature as those with a petrosiliceous base, or a base of felt spar in one mass*.

ACHNA-

---

* Deodat Dolomieu, who has so well observed the different causes which tend to decompose or discolour lavas, thinks with me, that there are some of them naturally white. " There are a number of lavas," says this learned mineralogist, " of a white or whitish colour, which have
" never been attacked by vapours, and which have not
" sustained the least alteration. This is proved by local
" circumstances, by the hardness, and the perfect preser-
" vation of the felt spar and the micas which they contain.
" I could instance a vast number of lavas which are na-
" tually

ACHNACREGS.

Beds of Lime-ftone, between two Banks of Free-ftone, in the midft of the Lavas, and with Belemnites in the Lime-ftone.

About half a mile from Achnacregs, and at no great diftance from the proftrate column which I have mentioned, and which the inhabitants regard as the work of Offian, there is by the fea-fide a craggy ridge, upon which the waves beat with fo much fury, that they have torn the volcanic rock in feveral directions.

By inceffantly attacking this natural mound, for fo many ages, the waves have brought to view a bed of lime-ftone, that formerly lay buried under a current of black bafaltic lava, of which the whole coaft is formed. This bed, which is at a medium, about fifteen feet broad, is completely uncovered for a fpace of at leaft twenty toifes in length at low water; and lofes itfelf in the mafs of lavas which rife into hills as they recede from the coaft.

" turally white; fuch are thofe of the Euganean moun-
" tains near Padua, named *granitello*, feveral lavas of Ætna,
" Germany, &c." Memoirs on the iflands of Ponces, by Deodat Dolomieu, Paris, Archet, 1788, in 8vo. p. 37.

The

The lime-ftone is grey, hard, and brittle. It is not very pure, being mixed with a fmall quantity of argillaceous earth; it is good, however, for making lime. I found fome belemnites in it, the largeft of which were five inches in length, and an inch and a half in circumference towards the bafe.

This calcareous ftratum does not adhere directly to the bafaltic lava. There is an intermedium of two pretty thick beds of quartzofe free-ftone with large grains, united by a cement partly calcareous. It is to thefe that the lava adheres; and had not the free-ftone been uncovered by the daily and violent action of the fea, it would never have been imagined that there exifted under thefe enormous maffes of bafaltic lava, a layer of calcareous matter, inclofed itfelf between two beds of free-ftone *.

---

* In the 160th and following pages of my Mineralogy of Volcanos, I have mentioned fome analogous, but much more remarkable appearances, which I obferved in the mountains of Chamarelle in Vivarais, near Villeneuve de Berg, where there are beds of lime-ftone and bafaltic lavas placed in alternate fucceffion, and where belemnites are found in the lime-ftone, as in that of Achnacregs In that work I have ftated my conjectures refpecting the manner in which thefe different beds might have been formed at the remote period when every part of the ocean was agitated by volcanos.

Grand.

Grand natural bafaltic Wall refembling an ancient Circus.

To the north of Achnacregs, on the right fide of the road from the houfe, and about fix hundred toifes diſtant from it, we obſerved, cloſe by the fea, a natural platform of a femi-circular ſhape, fituated on an eminence which riſes about a hundred and fifty feet above the level of the water, and which is entirely compoſed of black lavas of a bafaltic nature. This ſmall plain, which has a gentle ſlope, is bounded on the fouth by a perpendicular volcanic cliff.

A vaſt detached wall lines a portion of the circle, formed by a bafaltic rock which riſes in the oppoſite quarter, and there thence reſults a kind of antique circus that fills one with aſtoniſhment at the firſt glance, and gives this fingular place the appearance of a ruin as extraordinary as picturefque.

The objects aſſume a new character of grandeur in proportion as they are approached; and the picture becomes more ſtriking when the height of the wall and its aſtoniſhing regularity are viewed from a near fituation.

At

At firft, one is loft in confidering how, or from what motive, human beings fhould have raifed, in a place fo remote and defert, a monument prefenting the image of a Roman circus.

The farther the obferver advances, the more furprifing does this kind of arena become. A large angular breach in the midft of the wall permits the eye to difcover the interior of this antique ruin. On approaching the opening he feels a lively curiofity intermixed with uncertainty, refpecting the nature of the object prefented to his view. Such at leaft were the fenfations that my companions and myfelf experienced the firft time that we went to fee this remarkable place, which we conceived, even when quite clofe to it, to be a monument of art.

There is nothing here, however, but the work of nature, and one of the moft extraordinary productions of fubterraneous combuftion; no lefs aftonifhing, perhaps, in its kind, than that which gave exiftence to the cave of Fingal.

I have mentioned, that a rock of black bafaltes, cut perpendicularly down, and defcribing a natural fegment of a circle, forms

the

the bottom of the circus. A vaſt wall, perfectly upright, forms the remainder of the inclofure.

This wonderful wall engroſſed all our attention. It is eighty-nine feet long, perfectly ſtraight, and compofed entirely of prifms of black bafaltes, of equal length, and placed horizontally above each other; that is, all thefe prifms, which are in good prefervation, and pretty equal, laid one upon another, form the thickneſs of this wall which is detached on both fides. Its facings are pretty even, and it ſtands erect without any buttrefs, though it exceeds twenty-five feet in height. It is connected, at its northern entremity only, with a projecting part of the volcanic rock which forms the circular bottom of the amphitheatre.

The breach in the middle of the wall is fourteen feet four inches wide at bottom, that is, even with the ground, and forty feet at the top. It forms a large obtufe angle, and give a very picturefque appearance of a ruin to the whole of the circus. This opening is probably the effect of an earthquake. I counted about forty prifms within the wall which feemed to have belonged to it, and
about

about thirty-nine without. But thefe are nothing to what would be ftill neceffary to fill it up; and it is not very probable that any perfon carried them away. The fea is at prefent a hundred feet diftant from the wall, and forty feet lower than it. It is poffible, however, that the waves may have beat out the part at fome very remote period, and carried off the greater portion of the materials which are wanting. This conjecture, will perhaps, appear more probable than the firft, when I fhall have defcribed other objects in the vicinity of the wall, which are well fitted to throw fome light on the theory of its formation. I fhall fhortly return to this fubject.

Nothing is better calculated to convey an idea of this bafaltic wall than the manner in which the wood for firing is arranged in the wood-yards of Paris. It is well known that thefe pieces are all of the fame length, and that they are piled up horizontally above each other. I do not mean thofe enormous piles which over top the houfes, and form vaft maffes of wood; becaufe, in that cafe, the pieces are placed longitudinally and croffwife alternately, but I mean thofe kinds of walls: the thicknefs of which confift of the length of a

fingle

fingle piece, and which are carried only to the height of ten or twelve feet, that the wood may be more at hand for daily fale.

I am obliged to ufe this trivial comparifon, in order to make myfelf better underftood. It is not eafy to be perfpicuous, and at the fame time to avoid fatiguing the reader with details too minute or imperfectly expreffed, when it is neceffary to defcribe objects which Nature feems to have produced in her capricious moments, to embarrafs us with aberrations of which fhe exhibits a few examples only.

I am fully confcious of my inability to exprefs all that I faw, or all that I felt, on feeing the volcanic circus in the vicinity of Achnacregs. I therefore entreat the moft ample indulgence with refpect to what I have already faid, and what I have yet to obferve.

The height of the great wall is twenty-five feet ten inches, its thicknefs feven feet ten inches, and the prifms, of which it is compofed, are confequently of the fame length.

The prifms are pentagonal, hexagonal and feven fided. A very few are quadrangular; but the moft common are the pentagonal and hexagonal. They are black, hard, found in their fracture, and magnetic.

The firſt eight courſes of the upper part of the wall are formed of priſms of the ſame ſhape and ſize, in excellent preſervation, and placed horizontally one above another without any adheſion; that is, they might be eaſily raiſed one after another. But they lie ſo cloſe upon each other that there is no vacancy between them except merely the lines of ſeparation which define the priſms, and give the facings of this ſingular wall a reſemblance to moſaic work.

The priſms which ſucceed the firſt eight courſes are likewiſe of the ſame mould; but they are cut tranſverſely in ſome parts, either from the natural effect of contraction at the time of the lava's cooling, or from the weight of the incumbent maſs at a period long ſubſequent to their formation.

The wall commences towards the weſt, where it ſupports itſelf againſt a rock of lava. It then takes a ſouth-eaſt direction, and turning, ſtretches along to the north-north-weſt, and afterward to the ſouth-ſouth-eaſt. It is not of an equal height throughout. The higheſt part, which is alſo the beſt preſerved, is twenty-five feet ten inches, as I have ſtated already; the other parts are about twenty-

one

one feet feven inches high. It is detached on both fides, and is, in all, eighty-nine feet in length, including the breach. The greateft diameter of the circus, which is rather of an oval than circular form, is fixty-fix feet eight inches; and to bring all the meafurements into one view, I may repeat, that the wall is a hundred feet diftant from the fea, and ftands on a ground entirely covered with lava, and raifed forty feet above the level of the fea in ordinary tides.

It is doubtlefs very difficult to conceive how the lava, when flowing, could have formed a wall fo high, of fuch regular conftruction, unconnected with any other mafs, and compofed entirely of differently fided prifms, placed horizontally by the fide of each other, with fuch order and perfect fymmetry, that the art of the moft able ftone-cutter could never have arranged them with equal dexterity.

This problem, however, which is certainly attended with great difficulties, finds, on the fpot itfelf, fome means of folution, arifing from particular circumftances capable of conveying fome idea of the manner in which this prifmatic wall was formed.

For this purpofe, it is neceffary only to ftep about forty paces towards the fouth-foutheaft part of the circus, which is clofe by the fea. There two facts may be difcovered, which ferve to explain this remarkable theory.

I am happy that I continued fo long on the fpot, and that I fo carefully traced all the windings of this fingular volcanic monument; for, otherwife, this important obfervation might have efcaped me.

Two extenfive excavations naturally formed in the lava itfelf, one of which is twenty-two feet deep, fixteen feet broad, and a hundred and forty-fix feet long, and the other eighty-five long, nineteen broad, and twenty-one deep, at a medium, feem as if they had been defignedly placed there, at no great diftance from each other, to invite the obferver to repair thither in order to learn the manner in which nature operates in the conftruction of fuch walls.

Let the reader imagine to himfelf, for a moment, two ftreams of lava of a confiderable thicknefs, which at the time of fome great eruption, have flowed parallel to each other, with an interval of feveral toifes
between

between them: The case is not without a precedent, at Ætna, the volcano of the isle of Bourbon, and elsewhere. From these two streams result a long and deep gallery, or a kind of covert-way, more or less straight, more or less circular or winding, according to local circumstances, and the obstacles which might have occurred in their progress.

But admitting that two currents of lava might, by approaching each other, form a gallery, still it may be asked, how is it possible that they should assume a direction so equal and so parallel as to produce a channel nearly uniform throughout, and of which the interior surface is perfectly even? I might reply, that the case may have existed, since we have several instances of it, and I would add, that naturalists know very well, that in great eruptions, the lava does not flow along with the same fluidity as melted metals, but in the state of a thick paste, which the air, by cooling the parts exposed to its influence, consolidates in an erect position. This is a fact which may be witnessed in a number of instances, in which the boiling lava proceeds along slowly, but at the same time to a great distance, in a stream with per-

pendicular

pendicular fides. What is ftill more furprifing is, that thefe currents are fometimes feen to divide into two parts, like two branches of a river, on merely meeting with a body which one might fuppofe they could eafily overturn, fuch as a ftone mound, or even a houfe. Sir William Hamilton has accurately obferved, and defcribed this aftonifhing phenomenon in his excellent defcription of the eruption of Vefuvius.

Other caufes may contribute to give regularity and fmoothnefs to the interior facings of a gallery formed by two parallel currents of lava.

The volcano, for inftance, may have been fubmarine, or only in the vicinity of the fea, where thofe at prefent in activity are almoft all fituated. We have, then, only to fuppofe two currents of lava, flowing at a fmall diftance from each towards the water, and extending under it to a certain diftance. The fudden cooling, the refiftance of the fluid, the thick and deep flime which generally covers its bottom, a bank of fhifting fand, or other unknown caufes, may give rife to what fo much aftonifhes us, namely, the parallelifm and equality of the interior furface.

It

It is of little importance to know the exact and perfect theory of these works of nature. It is sufficient that the fact exists, and that it cannot be doubted, after examining the two large and deep galleries mentioned above, which appear in open view at no great distance from the circus, and which enable us to explain the formation of the great wall. I have only to entreat the readers' patience and indulgence for the details, already too long and tedious, which I am obliged to enter into in order to make myself intelligible upon a subject, dry and difficult in itself, but calculated to entertain with curious facts such as are attached to these kind of studies and observations.

The first of the two galleries was such as strongly to excite our attention at first fight. I have already said that it is eighty-five feet long, nineteen broad, and twenty-one feet of average depth. It is wholly uncovered. There is no access to it, however, except at one place, where, with a little address, and by the aid of some blocks of lava which have fallen in and form a kind of steps, one may descend to the bottom.

This

This long and profound excavation is the effect simply of two currents proceeding in the same direction, with an interval of fifteen feet between them. The lava of which they are compofed is black, and of the kind which I have denominated in the *Mineralogy of Volcanos*, gravelly lava; that is, which has little adhefion and falls naturally into gravelly fplinters, in the form of knobs of a greater or fmaller bulk having a general tendency to feparate in that manner, particularly in the parts expofed to the air and to the alternate effects of drynefs and humidity.

Matters being in this ftate, and the channel or gallery being formed, it then ferved as a mould to a current of bafaltic lava, compact, homogeneous, and of great folidity, which fubfequently flowed into it, and thus created a wall fomething fimilar to the cafed walls of the Romans.

As the current of bafaltic lava would pour along the channel in a boiling ftate, its fides, that is, the parts in contact with the faces of the gallery muft have neceffarily been the firft cooled. The caloric thus efcaping by the fides, the lava would fhrink into a fmaller bulk and muft thence have unavoidably cracked

into

into pieces of a prifmatic form. The lofs of heat, and the *gafeous* emanations forcing the matter to contract itfelf, the refult muft have been that this fort of caft wall fhould fplit into horizontal prifms of feveral fides, placed naturally one above another.

The outer walls, which ferved as moulds, and which are compofed of a gravelly earth, need only have been attacked and deftroyed by the water, either gradually during a lapfe of time, or by fome extraordinary agitation of the fea; and the middle wall, which confifted of the moft folid materials, being thus ftripped of its mould, would appear to have been erected in a miraculous manner, and to have arifen out of the earth as an amphitheatrical decoration.

This is precifely what happened in the prefent cafe, at leaft to fuch a degree as to admit of no doubt refpecting the fact: For, in the middle of the gallery I have mentioned, there appears a perpendicular wall, three and a half feet thick, and eight high, completely divefted of lava, detached on both fides, and entirely compofed of prifmatic columns laid horizontally above each other, but preferving a certain mutual adhefion, which has prevented

vented them from falling, and enabled them to refift the action of time and the elements, which they could not otherwife have withftood.

I thought I fhould never weary of admiring this wall. I could walk round it with eafe; the whole breadth of the gallery being only nineteen feet, of which the prifmatic wall occupied only four and a half; fo that it ftands nearly in the midft of a vacant fpace of fourteen feet fix inches, having feven feet three inches on each fide.

This vacancy was probably once filled up with the fame gravelly lava of which the fides of the gallery confift. The fea, which rufhes into the gallery with violence during tempeftuous weather and fpring tides, by an aperture which communicates with it, muft have carried off the gravellous lava wanting, and and in the center of which the wall was inclofed.

It is probable that from the continued action of time, rain, hoar-froft, and the fea, on the gravelly lava of the gallery, the wall will one day be entirely ftripped of any inclofure on either fide, and that no veftige will remain of the primitive mould to which it owes its formation.

I have

I have now only to mention its prefent height, which is no more than eight feet, whilft that of the cavity in which it is placed is twenty-one feet.

I reflected upon this fact on the fpot, and I think I fhall be able to account for it by faying, that it is probable that the wall was once higher, but that the upper courfes having been formed of prifms which did not adhere to each other, the fea muft have undermined and carried them away.

This opinion gains fome ftrength, from an examination of the fecond gallery, which is at a fmall diftance from the firft, and on which I fhall dwell for a moment only.

This gallery, which is much larger than the other, is a hundred and forty-fix feet long, twenty-two feet deep, and fixteen feet broad. It may be regarded, in one fenfe, at leaft, as the reverfe of the former. The two parallel currents, which have ferved to form it, confift of black, compact, very hard lava, in a folid mafs, which has refifted all the injuries of the weather, the action of the air, and the higheft tides.

A ftream of compact, homogeneous, lava, occupied alfo the whole length of this vaft gallery.

gallery. But the basaltic lava of this secondary current consisted of a paste so smooth and so well amalgamated, and which had so great a tendency to divide into regular and perfect, that they lay horizontally upon each other without any connection or adhesion between them, as far as I could judge from a small part of it remaining towards the beginning of the gallery, which the sea had not yet reached.

The prisms of this remnant are truly astonishing from their excellent state of preservation and the complete regularity of their form. They seem as if they had been placed there with all the care and art of human hands: so very wonderful is the symmetry and perfection of their arrangement. There is not one of these prisms, picked up at random, which would not figure in a cabinet of natural history.

Their want of adhesion has been the cause of their gradual demolition; for the waves meeting the most obstinate resistance from the sides of the gallery, which are of unshaken solidity, directed all their fury against the prisms, which they easily undermined and dragged into the depth of the ocean. Thus has the prismatic wall

wall been entirely deftroyed, wh'lft the mould, which contribute to form it remains unimpaired.

Such is the manner in which volcanos, fo frequently the agents of deftruction, are able to create, or rather to imitate, by a fucceffion of accidental circumftances, productions which cannot be effected by mankind without much labour and a train of tedious and difficult means and combinations *.

From

---

* I made thefe obfervations on the fpot in the month of October, 1784. Deodat Dolomieu, three years afterwards, that is, in the month of July, 1787, on vifiting the ifles of Ponces difcovered a fimilar wall, but confifting of much fmaller prifms. As the comparifon may be interefting to Naturalifts, I fhall make ufe of the language of my friend: "The fmall bafaltes are very numerous in the ifles of Pon-
"ces. They are found in a multitude of places, but princi-
" pally in the rocks of Chiardiluna, to the left of the fubter-
" raneous gallery. There are thoufands of them on both
" fides of the fmall bay of St. Mary, efpecially on the
" mountain in the rear of the houfes. Thefe fmall prif-
" matic columns naturally fplit afunder and fall into the
" fea. Some of them are of the moft perfect regularity,
" and exhibit all the variety of forms of which they are
" fufceptible. They are feen in heaps of different forms,
" but more frequently piled horizontally on each other,
" and rifing above the ground in the form of walls which
" perfectly refemble thofe in the ancient fabricks called
" *opera reticulata*. Several rows or walls made of prifms
" nearly a foot long, rife one behind another."

Dolomieu

From the preceding obfervations it would appear that the grand wall which forms the volcanic circus of Achnacregs, can have no other than the fame origin. But as the flat tract on which it ftands is forty feet above the prefent level of the fea, and the wall itfelf is ftill twenty-five feet ten inches high, it muft follow that the fea has fallen fixty-five feet ten inches in that quarter, unlefs we fuppofe that the coaft has been elevated by the incalculable efforts of fome vaft fubterraneous explofion.

Mr. Anderfon, who travelled by command of the Englifh government, with a view to the fifheries, through feveral of the Hebrides, at the time I vifited them, told me, that he faw in the ifle of Iflay, a volcanic wall of the fame kind with that of Achnacregs, refpecting which I had given him fome details. He further informed me, that the wall commences to the weft of the ifland in a place called *Cove*; that it defcribes a diagonal line of three hundred paces long; that it is at leaft fifty feet

---

Dolomieu entertains the fame opinion with me refpecting the theory of thefe walls; he regards them as having been formed by inclofure in the interftices of the lava.

Memoire fur les ifles Ponces, by Deodat Dolomieu. Paris 1788, in 8vo. 98 and following pages.

high

high and four feet thick; that about one-half of it ſtands out of the water, and the other projects into the ſea, where it forms a jutty ſo extraordinary and ſo much reſembling the work of art, that, at the firſt view, it would appear to be the production of human labour.

CHAP.

CHAPTER VIII.

The Ifle of Kerrera.

THE ifles of Mull and Kerrera are feparated by a narrow channel which may be croffed from Achnacregs in lefs than four hours. Kerrera almoft touches the main land, by a point which runs out towards Oban; for the ftrait on that fide is in fome places not above fifty toifes broad. I croffed the ifle of Kerrera diagonally in order to get to a fmall ferry-boat, which was at one of its extremities.

A part of the ifland is volcanic. On the coaft fronting Mull there are collections of compact lavas difpofed in maffes and in large currents. This bafaltic lava appears fometimes in the form of prifms, which are not very regular, at leaft in the places which I had an opportunity of examining. I alfo found fome rocks of micaceous fchiftus of a whitifh colour, and others which were

greenifh

greenish with a fibrous texture. Thefe fchiftus or *kneifs* are compofed of quartz, fteatites and fmall fcales of mica.

Near the rocks of micaceous fchiftus there is found common flate of a deep grey colour, approaching to black, the beds of which are almoft even with the ground: quarries might be eafily opened here with great advantage to the country. They would even become an object of commerce. Among the flate there are found fome brilliant pyrites, the cryftalizations of which are cubical.

Such were the objects which engroffed my attention in the ifle of Kerrera, where I obferved a good deal of pafture ground, and fome cultivated parts bearing barley and oats. The cottages were fcattered to the right and left, but they were few in number.

I was only four hours in croffing the whole length of the ifland. I found at its extremity the ferry-boat which I mentioned above. It was a fmall fkiff managed by a fingle man. I was fatigued. I made the boatman proceed directly to Oban, where I landed in lefs than an hour, and I found

found Count Andreani with our carriages, and every thing ready for our departure on the next day. In the evening, we made every neceffary preparation for commencing our journey by day-break.

CHAP-

CHAPTER IX.

Departure from Oban.—Dalmally.—Tindrum.— Lead Ore.—Killin.—River Mufcle containing Pearls.—Defcription of thefe Pearls and their origin.

WE left Oban on the 7th of October, at fix in the morning, to proceed to Dalmally. The diftance is about twenty-four miles, along a ftony road, paffing through ravines. We arrived at the place of our deftination about feven in the evening.

Bunhave, of which I have already fpoken, is about midway; it is a fmall hamlet, built at the union of a branch of Loch Awe, with Loch Etive, which has fufficient water for, fmall veffels, and where falmon abounds.

We vifited an iron foundery, at a fmall diftance from Bunhave. It ftands in a charming fituation, embellifhed around with woods, verdant banks, and cultivated fields. A beautiful avenue led to the Loch, which was at this time covered with veffels, that
rendered

rendered the scene so much the more enchanting. This delightful spot formed a strong contrast with the barren mountains of reddish porphyry, and the piles of rocky fragments with which it is surrounded.

We were agreeably surprised to find an establishment of this kind in so distant a part of Scotland, where cultivation and the arts have made so little progress; we were informed that it belonged to an English company who had been induced to erect works in this place in consequence of the abundance of wood and water and its proximity to the sea.

We waited upon the manager of the works, who received us very politely, and shewed us some iron of a very fine quality, the result of his labours. I expressed my astonishment that this iron should be made in a place where there was no indication of ore, and observed to him, that I had not seen the smallest vestige of any all the way from Ob'n. He replied, that my surprise was very natural, for that the ore used in this foundery was brought in vessels from Cumberland; he then shewed me some collections of red hematites, partly decomposed, of an excellent quality and rich in iron.

This

This eſtabliſhment appeared to be conducted with equal ſkill and economy; but the wood was beginning to become ſcarce, as the neighbouring foreſts were not ſufficiently extenſive to yield conſtant and regular ſupplies. It is therefore to be feared that this foundery cannot be carried on much longer.

On arriving at Dalmally I had the pleaſure of ſeeing our good friend, Patrick Fraſer, who ſupped and paſſed the evening with us. He informed me of new reſearches he had made with reſpect to the poetry of Oſſian, ſome fragments of which he had recovered, in the different excurſions he made for that purpoſe among the inhabitants of the mountains, and little frequented places of this part of Scotland. He had alſo enriched his collection with other poems made by the more modern bards of the country. This worthy man, of a mild, modeſt character, and paſſionately fond of literature, was unfortunately placed like an exile in the midſt of theſe barren and melancholy mountains, where, to preſerve his exiſtence, he was obliged to perform the functions of a ſchoolmaſter. I earneſtly wiſh that his condition may be ameliorated. The Antiquarian Society, eſtabliſhed at Edinburgh, would

would do well to employ the knowledge and activity of Patrick Frafer in refearches refpect-ing the ancient ftate of fcience and literature in Scotland. He has the advantage of being perfectly mafter of the original language of his country, which has not the fmalleft relation to the Englifh.

Patrick Frafer begged that I would fend him fome French books which he wanted; and, on my return to Paris, I fhall haften to pay to him this fmall teftimony of my efteem for his talents, and refpect for his moral qualities *. " I can only," faid he, " in return, " give you my addrefs, and offer you my poor " fervices in this country." I here with pleafure tranfcribe this addrefs in Englifh, that thofe who may feel an intereft in knowing this affable and amiable man may not be ignorant of the place of his refidence. It was exactly as follows : " *Patrick Frafer,* " *Schoolmafter, of Glenorchy, by Inveraray,* " *Scotland.*"

* I have fent him fuch books as I thought would be agreeable to him; but the diftance and the difficulty of communication to this diftant part of Scotland, have, doubtlefs, prevented me from hearing from him; it is even poffible that he has neither received my letter, nor my packet.

We ſlept at Dalmally, and proceeded next morning to Tindrum; the journey was only twelve miles, but we wiſhed to arrive in time that we might have an opportunity of examining the lead ore which we were informed was to be ſeen in the neighbourhood of that place.

The valley of Glenlochy, through which we paſſed, is in ſome places very agreeable. It is ſkirted with hills which are covered with flocks of ſheep; but we found that the mountains cloſed as we advanced, and the ſoil became marſhy and ſterile. The turf with which it was covered, gave a very diſmal hue to the face of the country, which excited in our minds a ſenſation of correſponding melancholy.

The hamlet of Tindrum conſiſts of only a few houſes which are almoſt all detached; it ſtands upon a low marſhy piece of ground: a humid and unwholeſome vapour renders its ſituation very diſagreeable.

The place where the lead ore is found is not far diſtant from the iron, but it is very elevated. It is neceſſary to form the galleries in a very high mountain of difficult acceſs. They are cut through a grey micaceous ſchiſtus rock, which is intermixed with a

con-

confiderable quantity of white quartz: the vein of lead ore is found in a matrix of the latter fubftance. The ore is ufually accompanied by pyrites or horn-ftone, and it is fufficiently abundant. It is fometimes covered with fine cryftals of calcareous fpar. The galleries in general are in a very bad condition, and the works are very negligently managed.

When the pieces of ore are extracted they are broken with hammers, they are then wafhed to feparate the ore from foreign fubftances, which, when thus prepared, is tranfported to a foundery fituated in the valley at the bottom of the mountain: charcoal and turf are ufed in fmelting it; but I do not know in what proportion, becaufe the foundery was not worked at this time, on account of fome reparations which were then making in the furnace. Befides, the Englifh, as well as the Dutch, are very referved in explaining their proceffes, even in the moft fimple arts, which they always exercife with a kind of myftery: It is not fo in France; there the managers of the moft interefting eftablifhments, are in general very complaifant, and frankly communicate to a ftranger all the information he can defire.

I obferved

I obferved under vaft fheds confiderable piles of peats, and near them a heap of pit-coal. From this, I prefumed, that in ufing the peats, a mixture of a fourth or fifth part of coal is added. The latter article muft be carefully hufbanded, on account of the diftance of the pits, and the dearnefs of land-carriage.

It would be defireable for the benefit of our manufactories in which wood begins to be fcarce, that a fimilar mixture of peat and coal fhould be employed, where they can be procured. As I fhould have been happy to fupport my recommendation with an example, I begged of one of the fuperintendants of the works to inform me in what proportions the peat and coal were ufed; but he turned a deaf ear to my requeft, and changed the converfation to fome other topic.

It is very eafy, however, to make experiments upon the fubject, and there is no doubt of their being attended with fuccefs; particularly if conducted by perfons well acquainted with the quality of the peat and turf which are to be ufed.

It appears that the lead-mines of Tindrum have formerly been much more productive and valuable.

I left

I left this place and proceeded to Killin, by a road as difmal as uniform in its appearance. I much doubt whether another fuch can be found. It is made upon a bottom of fpungy turf, which permits the water to filtrate eafily through its elaftic and moving fubftance, without however becoming marfhy, for carriages pafs over it without any inconvenience.

But what renders it moft infupportably tirefome is, that it extends in this ftate for feveral leagues, between two clofe mountains, covered with a black turf, on which there grow nothing but fhort heath and fome yellowifh moffes, that diftil the water, drop by drop, on all fides.

The mind foon participates in the gloomy hue, and is more and more overcaft with fadnefs, as the traveller advances; but on reaching the extremity of this kind of fombre gallery, the fcene is fuddenly changed, the horizon expands, and the fine valley of *Glen Dochart*, fucceeded by that of *Strafilan*, open to his view.

Here limpid and copious ftreams, teeming with fifh, glide in ferpentine meanders, through the fmiling verdure, and form iflets

fhaded

shaded with wide spreading trees. On every side appear neat rustic habitations, with numerous flocks of black cattle and sheep, and the young shepherds and shepherdesses who tend them make the air resound with their songs, and animate the delightful scene with their dances.

This day we rode twenty-four miles at our full ease, and reached Killin before night.

Killin, though called a town, is in fact nothing more than a hamlet, consisting of a few scattered houses at the extremity of Loch Tay. The inn is very plain in its appearance, but its accommodations are tolerably good, and the landlord is a very civil man. Over the chimney-piece of a small parlour hung several native birds, which himself had carefully stuffed with straw, among others a white wood-cock, which William Thornton purchased, as he also did some heath-cocks.

We were about sitting down to table, when I was surprized with hearing a stranger, who wished to speak with me, call me by my name: I soon perceived from his manner and his language that he was a Frenchman; his person also was somewhat known to me. I told him

him that I thought I had seen him in Paris, but that I could not at the moment recollect who it was that I had the honour of addressing. " I am Bombelles," said he ; " I " travel like yourself, for pleasure and in- " struction. I am now on my way to *Port* " *Patrick*, where I design to embark for Ire- " land." It was from one of our servants that he heard of my being in the inn, where he had just arrived himself in one of Lord Bredalbane's carriages, at whose house he had gone to spend a few days.

I had never had any intimacy with M. de Bombelles. But two Frenchmen who meet each other in the wilds of Scotland are not long in forming an acquaintance ; and we had besides several common friends. From the course which M. de Bombelles pursued, as well as from a number of military and other charts which he had along with him, I judged that diplomacy and politics were more suitable to his taste than the natural sciences or the arts, and that he was probably charged with some particular mission, very foreign from the object of my studies. I ought, however, to do M. de Bombelles's talents and activity the justice to say, that he neglected
nothing

nothing which was in any degree interefting to his country. This I had an opportunity of judging from fome oftenfible parts of a well-written journal, which he communicated to me at the time, and in which I faw feveral articles relative to rural economy and commerce, and likewife a curious phyfical fact refpecting a very extraordinary flux and reflux, which had been recently feen in Loch Tay. I had already heard it mentioned in the Duke of Argyle's, at Inveraray; and M. de Bombelles, during his ftay at Lord Bredalbane's, which is clofe to the lake, received the beft information that could be procured on the fubject. I fhall here infert the note which he gave me, as it ferved to direct my enquiries when I vifited the place on the following day.

" Between the hours of eight and nine in the
" morning of the 12th of September (1784)
" the water of the eaftern part of Loch Tay
" retreated to the diftance of more than three
" hundred feet from its ordinary limits, and
" the whole of that fpace, in which it was
" generally three feet deep, was left quite
" dry. The water on leaving it, ebbed to-
" wards the weft, but met with a contrary
" wave,

"wave, when the violence of the shock
"raised both to the height of four feet, ac-
"companied with much foam. The waters
"thus rushing in oppofite directions, formed
"by their junction one vaft wave, which
"moved towards the fouth, ftill preferving
"a height of more than four feet above the
"level of the lake, and remained in that
"ftate nearly ten minutes. This extraordi-
"nary tide then began to fubfide gradually,
"and in about an hour and a half entirely
"difappeared. It is very fingular, that during
"this phenomenon, the fky was perfectly
"ferene, and the air calm, and that there
"was no perceptible motion at the oppofite
"extremity of the lake. Two days after,
"the fame appearance recurred; but one
"hour later, and not in fo remarkable a de-
"gree."—*Note extracted from the Journal
of M. de Bombelles, 9th of October* 1784.

M. de Bombelles * took the road to Inveraray; whilft I made a little longer ftay at
Killin, to procure as much information as poffible relative to the pearl-fifhery of the river

---

* This is the perfon who was fhortly after appointed
Ambaffador to Portugal.

Tay,

Tay, which here falls into the lake, to which it gives name.

The master of the inn, who obligingly exerted himself respecting every thing that could gratify my curiosity, brought me two fishers, whose particular employment was searching for pearls.

They conducted us to the river which runs in a very pure stream upon a bottom of sand or pebbles, and they soon brought up several dozens of shells, from three and a half to four inches long, and a little more than two inches broad; their exterior colour was a deep brown, inclining a little to green. The upper shell was thick, and of a fine mother-of-pearl colour within, slightly tinged with rose colour. I regarded this species as belonging to the *mia pictorum* of Linæus, or at least, as very nearly resembling it.

The fishers, in consideration of a handsome reward, which we promised them, engaged to open these shells in our presence upon the bank. But they stipulated for the reservation of the pearls, if any should be found, that they might sell them to us at a separate price; and to this proposition we acceded.

Imagining

Imagining from this that we fhould put a higher value on thofe which might be found, while we were prefent; thefe artful practitioners brought with them fome pearls, which they dexteroufly introduced into feveral of the fhells in opening them. They appeared to be well exercifed in this petty fort of impofition, which, however, I detected in a manner that aftonifhed and perplexed them, and that deferves to be mentioned, as it depended upon a memorable fact with regard to one of the caufes which contribute to the formation of pearls.

I defired them to open the mufcles before my fellow-travellers, whilft I went to amufe myfelf with fifhing fome of them; but they were to inform me when they difcovered any pearls. I was foon called and fhewn a very fine pearl, perfectly round, and of a good colour. I looked at the fhell and the pearl, and then told them, that the latter was not found in the mufcle fhewed me. The fifhers affured me that it was, and appealed to the teftimony of my companions, who confirmed their affertion. I affured the latter, however, that they were deceived, and begged them to watch more narrowly the next time.

time. I retired a few steps, and a minute or two after I heard one exclaim, we have found another. I went up, and on examining the mufcle, I pronounced that the pearl had, for that time alfo, been flipped into the fhell. The pearl was beautiful; but the price which they demanded for it was fix times its value.

The fifhers exhibited the utmoft degree of aftonifhment; for, as I was at fome diftance from them, it was clear that I could not have obferved their motions; my fellow-travellers who attentively watched them, were themfelves deceived, or at moft entertained only a vague fufpicion; fo well fkilled were thefe men in an art which procured them a few additional fhillings from travellers.

My art was fo fupernatural in their eftimation, that they confeffed the impofition, and frankly fhewed us fome other pearls which they had in referve for the fame purpofe. They were very anxious to learn my fecret, which would fave them the pains of frequently opening a vaft number of fhells to no purpofe, for they feldom found above one or two pearls in a week. But as they knew no other language than the Earfe, and not even fo much as a word of Englifh, I could explain myfelf myself only by signs and gestures; and, though my instructions were not very difficult, I doubt whether they were completely intelligible in a conversation of this sort.

My secret consisted merely in examining attentively the outside of the muscles, and when neither of the parts had any cavity or perforation, but presented a surface smooth and free from callosities, I could pronounce, without any apprehension of being deceived, that there was no pearl in such a shell. If, on the contrary, the shell was pierced with auger-worms, and indented by other worms of the same kind, there were always found pearls more or less valuable, or, at least the embryons of pearls.

This observation, which I have found invariably true hitherto, was the result of some enquiries, in which I had been engaged a long time before, respecting the formation of that beautiful animal product. Bouffon introduces the information, which I communicated to him upon this subject, in his article upon pearls, page 125, vol. iv. of the *Natural History of Minerals*. At that time I discovered that the pearl fish is attacked by two classes of enemies. One is a very small auger-
worm,

worm, which penetrates into the infide, near the edge of the valve, by working a longitudinal paffage between the different laminæ that compofe the cover. This fmall channel, on extending to an inch or an inch and a half in length, doubles back in a line parallel to the firft, and feparated from it by a very thin partition of fhelly matter. Thefe two parallel lines difcover the direction of the worm in entering and returning; which is alfo very diftinguifhable on the furface by two fmall holes, clofe to the edge, and in general near the mouth of the fhell.

The parallelifm of the two paffages may be demonftrated by introducing a pin into each orifice. At the inner extremity, however, there is a fmall circular portion, formed by the worm in turning round.

As thefe fmall channels or covert-ways are excavated in the part neareft the mother-of-pearl, or filvery internal coat, the pearly juice foon extravafates and produces protuberances in that direction. The cylindrical bodies thus formed may be confidered as elongated pearls, adhering to the internal lining of the fhell. When feveral worms of this kind penetrate near each other, and unite their labours, the

M 2 refult

result is a sort of pearly wen, with irregular protuberances, in which the issues of the passages which they have formed are easily distinguishable.

Another sea-worm, much larger, and of the family of the multivalvous shell-fish, attacks the pearl shells in a much more ingenious manner. This worm is a pholas of the species of sea dates. I have in my cabinet an oyster from the coast of Guinea, pierced by one of these pholades, which are still as they were found in the heel of the oyster. The shells of these singular pholades are hinged in the form of a crooked bill. The small hole which they bore resembles the figure of a pear; and pearls of this shape are sometimes found, which were in high estimation among the ancients, and are at present very valuable in the East-Indies: I shall give a more particular description of this rare species of pholades' in another work.

There are undoubtedly several other kinds of worms which pierce the pearl shell, and form cavities more or less round, in which the juice consolidates into pearls.

It is this observation which has no doubt been made by others besides me, that probably

first

firſt ſuggeſted to ſome perſons concerned in the pearl fiſhery, the trick of making artificial perforations in the ſhells, and thus forcing them to produce pearls. At London I ſaw ſome ſhells brought from China, which muſt have undergone this operation: for the artificial hole was filied up with a piece of braſs wire, rivetted on the outſide of the ſhell like the head of a nail, and the part of the wire which pierced the interior ſhining coat, was covered with a well ſhaped pearl, which ſeemed as if ſoldered to its extremity. It is probable, that, with the Chineſe, who have been ſo long skilled in the arts, and whoſe aſtoniſhing and multiplied induſtry teaches us, that we are but a comparatively new people, this is not a diſcovery of very modern date.

Brouſſonet, with whom I had a converſation upon this ſubject in London, at the houſe of Sir Joſeph Banks, told me, that a perſon had aſſured him, that there is ſtill another method of obtaining pearls. The ſhell on which the experiment is to be made, muſt be opened with the greateſt care in order to prevent the animal from being injured. A ſmall portion

portion of the inner furface is then fcraped off, and in its room is inferted a fpherical piece of mother-of-pearl about the fize of a very fmall grain of lead-fhot. This globule ferves as a nucleus to the pearly juice, which concretes around it, and at a certain diftance of time, produces a fine pearl. He faid, that experiments of this nature had been tried in Finland, and repeated alfo in other countries.

From thefe obfervations it may be inferred that the production of pearls depends, perhaps, much more upon an external and accidental caufe, than upon a natural fuperabundance or extravafation of the juice of which they are formed.

There are very excellent pearls found in the river fhells of Loch Tay, if we may judge from fome which the fifhers of Killin offered to fell us, at more than double the price of thofe which are in current fale. But thefe fine pearls are far from numerous; on the contrary, a very great number are found, which the jewellers reject, but which, though they may be not well calculated to form decorations for the ladies, are yet very interefting

ing for the cabinet of the Naturalift, fince they afford a confirmation of the theory which I have now mentioned. The greater part of thefe pearls have little or no luftre; fome are round, oval, or elongated and cylindrical; others are hemifpherical and refemble a button; feveral oblong ones have a contraction towards the middle which gives them the appearance of two joined together; others alfo are fomewhat conical; and all are of a pretty large fize, and of a pale red or brown colour. The end of the pearl touching the tegument of the fhell which forms what is called mother-of-pearl, is fo deeply impregnated with the fhining fubftance, that it exhibits a fingular contraft with the furrounding brown colour of the other parts, and feems to derive additional fplendour from it. This coating is of an orient bordering on rofe colour, which is extremely agreeable to the eye, and is therefore heightened in its effect by the contraft.

Pearls of this kind are fo feldom met with, that they might at firft be taken for occulated agates prepared for being fet, or rather for *buffonites*, particularly thofe which have no mother-of-pearl. Their texture is very hard, and yields with great difficulty to the file.

The auger-worm, which occafions the formation of the pearls of Loch Tay, pierces the whole thicknefs of the fhell, which is of confiderable denfity and of a fallow brown colour; and as the fhelly juice oozes out from all parts of the orifice which the worm has formed, it neceffarily refults that the pearl muft participate in the quality and colour of the fubftance of the fhell, from the exterior layer to that which lines and embellifhes its inner furface.

Hence originate thofe rude but fingular gems above-mentioned, which have only a thin coating of mother-of-pearl upon one fide. There are, however, fome inftances in which the pearl is pure and brilliant throughout; proceeding, probably, from an extravafion of the interior coating only; which may have been occafioned by another kind of auger-worm attacking the fhell folely in the direction of that coating. It is the province of thofe Naturalifts, whofe at-

tention

ENGLAND AND SCOTLAND.   169

tention it has more particularly engaged, to inveſtigate more profoundly this very intereſting ſubject, our knowledge of which muſt yet be confidered as nothing more than a rude outline.

CHAP-

CHAPTER X.

Kenmore.—Extraordinary Flux and Reflux of Loch Tay.

W now took leave of the pearl fishers and our landlord, who obligingly gave us all the information in his power, and proceeded on our way to Kenmore, along the left bank of the Tay, which is skirted on both sides by granitic mountains, that confine the view within a very narrow compass. The foot of the mountains is tolerably well cultivated; but the only produce is oats, which are not reaped till about the middle of October. These oats a very tall; they were only beginning to be cut down at the time I passed; I measured several stalks, and found the shortest to be four feet high, and the longest five feet six inches *.

The

---

* I do not entirely agree with Knox, who visited this place sometime after me, when he says, " that its banks " on both sides are fruitful, populous, and finely diversi- " fied by the windings of the lake, and the various ap- " pearances of the mountains." The views upon both
sides

The lake is about fourteen miles long, and about a mile of mean breadth. I had no certain information of its depth*. It abounds in fiſh, and its waters are ſoft and clear.

The mountains which are neareſt the lake, and encloſe it on all ſides, are compoſed of a ſchiſtus micaceous rock, intermixed with felt ſpar and quartzoſe matter; the latter is moſt abundant. In this rock I found a few garnets, of a bad configuration and coarſe texture.

On reaching the ſouthern extremity of Loch Tay, we found on a very agreeable ſpot a commodious inn, ſeveral private habitations, a new-built church, and a bridge thrown over a ſmall river which iſſues from the lake; the whole is ſurrounded with trees, which enliven this fine little landſcape. The name of the place is Kenmore.

Here the traveller begins to perceive that he approaches the open country, and is ſoon to emerge from the barren mountains of the

ſides are too confined, and exhibit only the ſame dreary aſpect, and a few ſcattered patches of oats, preſent only the image of an ungrateful ſoil.

* The ſame author, ſpeaking of the depth of the lake, ſays, " that it varies from fifteen to a hundred fathoms;" this appears to me very extraordinary.

north

north of Scotland The air which he inhales, the cultivated face of the foil, the encreafing number of inhabitants, every thing conveys the intelligence; and this firft gradation of change fills his foul with a fentment of mild delight, which I cannot better exprefs, than by comparing it to that which we feel on the return of fpring, though at this time it was the end of autumn. But it might be faid that all was wintry, wild, dreary and fterile in the region which I had traverfed.

My firft care, on arriving at Kenmore, was to procure the moft exact accounts refpecting the flux and reflux of the lake, which happened on the 12th of the preceding September; as it was near this that the phenomenon firft took place, and it was here, therefore, that it could have been obferved with moft advantage.

The mafter of the inn to whom I applied for information, and who underftood Englifh, tranfported with the reputation which that event had conferred on the place of his refidence, conceived that I had come from France, for the exprefs purpofe of feeing a country, which was, in his opinion, fo juftly deferving of celebrity. He, accordingly,

gave

gave me the moſt cordial reception, for which I feel pleaſure in this opportunity of expreſſing my grateful acknowledgment.

"I cannot myſelf," ſaid he, "have the pleaſure of explaining how, what you wiſh to be informed of, happened, becauſe I was abſent from home, on the firſt day of the lake's motion. But I can direct you to two perſons who ſaw, and attended to, the whole of its progreſs, and who will ſhew on the ſpot how it proceeded. One of them, in particular, who is a lad of ſome acuteneſs, has carefully obſerved all the facts; and you will have reaſon to be ſatisfied with what he may tell you. You may, however, examine both; I ſhall go and order them to accompany you, and to anſwer all your enquiries; for they are both my ſervants."

The one was called James Allan, the other John M'Kenzie. The latter was the younger of the two; but he ſeemed to poſſeſs a greater portion of intelligence, and a ſpirit of obſervation more rational, and leſs diſpoſed to the admiſſion of the marvellous than his comrade.

M'Kenzie

M'Kenzie told me, that at nine of the morning of the 12th of September, the fky being ferene and the air calm, a peafant who had gone to wafh his hands in the part of the lake where the river iffues, obferved the water leaving the bank in a very perceptible manner, which obliged him to advance a few paces farther; but it ftill continued to retreat from him. This appearance gave him fo much furprize, that he haftened to inform his neighbours of it; one of whom then told him, that, at fun-rife, having heard a noife fimilar to that of a fudden blaft of wind, he went to the window, when, to his no fmall aftonifhment, he perceived the water receding from its banks, as if acted on by the impulfe of a violent hurricane; but finding the air perfectly calm, his aftonifhment rofe to the higheft degree.

M'Kenzie having told me that he had thefe accounts from the peafant, I requefted to fee the latter. He was immediately fent for, but he had previoufly fet out for a village fix miles off. Having, therefore, had no opportunity of converfing with him myfelf, the details which I am to communicate, cannot be delivered as pofitive facts. Peafants being in general ftrongly inclined to the

mar-

marvellous, the noife, which, according to his account, preceded the ebbing of the waters, appeared to me fomewhat apocryphal. M'Kenzie entertained the fame opinion.

The latter, continuing his relation, faid that he was not informed of this extraordinary motion of the lake until ten of the morning on which it firft appeared. He inftantly repaired to the brink of the lake, where he remained more than an hour and a half, obferving the facts as they occurred with the moft minute attention. During this period, he plainly faw the water ebb and flow ten times fucceffively; and the fame alternate motion continued for the whole of that day.

He communicated to me all thefe circumftances on the edge of the lake, and on the fame fpot upon which he ftood when making his obfervations. He pointed out a large ftone pretty far in the water, as the limit of its retreat.

As this part of the lake was little more than three feet in depth, I caufed the fpace between the ftone and the water's edge to be carefully meafured, and found it one hundred and fifty French feet. But John M'Kenzie

did

did not omit to inform me, that when the phenomenon happened, the water was not fo high upon the bank by eight feet. To prove this, he pointed to a ſtake which he had driven into the ground at the level at which it then ſtood, and which was about eight feet below its preſent margin. The exact meaſurement, therefore, of the ſpace abandoned by the water, was one hundred and fifty-two feet. From this, it ſhould ſeem that the account which M. de Bombelles received at Lord Bredalbane's, ſtating this ſpace at three hundred feet, requires to be corrected. It ought, indeed, to be obſerved, that as M'Kenzie was not on the ſpot until an hour after the water began to move, it is not improbable that the firſt impulſe, which he did not ſee, might have been much ſtronger, than thoſe which ſucceeded it. But as there is no proof to ſupport this ſuppoſition, whilſt the fact which fell under M'Kenzie's obſervation is aſcertained by preciſe meaſurement, it is more adviſeable to adopt his account.

The lake exhibited the ſame phenomenon on the following day, and likewiſe on the third day, but not in ſo frequent and regular a manner.

No body obferved its appearances in the night; nothing, therefore, is known of what happened during that time.

M'Kenzie faid, that during the ebb, the water receded from the bank without any violent or fudden agitation, but with the moft gentle motion, until it reached the large ftone, from which it returned to its former verge in the fame flow and gradual manner.

The inhabitants of Kenmore, whom I had accefs to confult, all agree with M'Kenzie in the following facts:

1ft. The motions of the lake during the fourth day, happened only at very diftant intervals. 2dly. On the fifth, fixth and feventh days, there was no ebb of the waters. 3dly. On the eighth, the motion appeared for a few hours only; and this was the cafe during two whole weeks, with intervals of two or three days, entirely motionlefs. 4thly. The motion abated gradually, and the lake refumed its former ftillnefs. 5thly. During the whole of this time, there was no violent wind, nor the flighteft fhock of earthquake.

These are the facts which are most deserving of credit, and I conceive it not improper to introduce them here, for the purpose of dispelling those additions of the marvellous, with which the English papers did not fail to embellish them. Having myself carefully collected the preceding accounts on the spot, they may be safely confided in. This is not a suitable place for entering into an examination of the causes which might have occasioned this wonderful flux and reflux in a lake where such a phenomenon had never occurred before. Similar phenomena have, indeed, taken place in other lakes. But we have not as yet a sufficient number of facts, and those which are already known have not been collected by persons sufficiently exercised in the difficult art of observation, to enable us to form any satisfactory speculations upon the subject.

We had scarcely left Kenmore on our way to Dunkeld, when we were agreeably surprized to find ourselves on a road bordered with fine Scottish and American pines, and other beautiful evergreens, kept in good order,

disposed

disposed with taste, and diffusing over the scene an attractive and enlivening appearance, which announced the vicinity of some great habitation.

About a mile farther, we came to the verge of a vast park, decorated with plantations of various kinds in the midst of verdant lawns, and divided through its whole length by the river Tay, over which are thrown two or three bridges of different constructions. Numerous herds of deer feed in this delightful place; sheep, fine looking beeves, and horses of various breeds, give the whole an air of abundance, usefulness, and taste, which display at once the enlarged mind and high fortune of the proprietor. A vast pile of building, partly in the gothic and partly in the modern style, closed this magnificent prospect. It is the residence of the Earl of Bredalbane.

I had heard so much praise of the character of this nobleman, whose chief occupation is to spread industry and happiness around him, that I was extremely sorry I had not procured a letter of introduction to him, with which the Duke of Argyle would have certainly obliged me, had I requested it.

it. But it did not form part of my original plan to pafs through Tindrum or Kenmore; on the contrary, it was my intention to return by Inveraray; and it was not until my fecond arrival at Dalmally, that I refolved to change the order of my journey, with the view of obtaining authentic accounts refpecting the ebb and flow of Loch Tay. I regret the lofs of this opportunity of acquiring a knowledge of the extenfive improvements in agriculture and rural economy, conducted with fo much fuccefs by the Earl of Bradelbane, and of becoming acquainted with a man who enjoys fo excellent a reputation, and is fo ufeful to his country.

We dined at a very good and commodious inn, about a mile from Dunkeld, oppofite to that agreeable little town, and built on eminence furrounded with woods and rocks. A vaft ruinous gothic church gives Dunkeld a very picturefque appearance.

We reached Perth a little late in the evening, by a road extremely rugged and fatiguing.

CHAPTER XI.

Perth, its Harbour and Manufactures.—Mr. M'Comie, Professor of Mathematics; Mr. M'Greggor, Professor of the French Language at the Academy.— Volcanic Mountain of Kinnoul.—The Agates found upon it.

THE small city of Perth stands in a very agreeable situation on the river Tay, which the tide enters to a considerable distance, and renders navigable for small vessels. It is in a pretty flourishing condition, and contains a population of about twelve thousand souls.

The stone bridge over the Tay was constructed by the same person who built that of Blackfriars, at London. It is very well executed, but is rather narrow for its length.

William Thornton had an acquaintance at Perth, of the name of M'Comie, who was professor of Mathematics in the college, which bears here the title of academy. We paid him a visit, and such was his goodness and complaisance, that he was constantly with us during our stay at Perth, where we remained

mained nearly a week. We derived the moſt
uſeful ſervices from him, as well as from one
of his colleagues, Mr. M'Gregor, profeſſor
of the French Language, who had received
his firſt education at Paris, and who was
kind enough alſo to favour us with his company, and to conduct us to ſeveral manufactories.

Before the reformation took place in England and Scotland, the town of Perth, where
the catholic worſhip reigned in all its ſplendor, contained ſome conſiderable religious
foundations, beſides a number of churches.
Of theſe, the greater part have ſince been
laid in ruins, or converted into churches for
the uſe of the preſbyterians. In ſeveral of
the ſtreets are ſeen ſome fine gothic facades,
which once belonged to cathedrals, chapterhouſes, monaſteries, and nunneries. Theſe
remains of monuments, conſecrated to a worſhip which formerly flouriſhed ſo vigorouſly
in the three kingdoms, announce that religions, as well as governments, have their periods of inſtability and revolution, which inceſſantly ſucceed each other at intervals of
longer or ſhorter extent, but which, when the
impulſe is once given, no human power is
able

able to arreft: So true is it, that in morals, as well as in phyfics, there is nothing durable in this world.

Machines for carding and fpinning cotton, had been introduced at Perth only a little before our arrival there. We faw the firft of them at the manufactory of an individual who had caufed them to be conftructed at Manchefter. He found it impoffible, however, to convey them out of that town but during the night; fo jealous are the manufacturers of Manchefter of this happy invention of Arkwright, which has given fuch extenfive celebrity and immenfe advantages to its commerce.

The moft confiderable manufactures of Perth are fine linen, thread, and flax; and fome very excellent articles are produced in this line. Here I faw a loom for weaving very large bed fheets, in one piece, by means of a fhuttle fixed on fmall rollers. A pair of thefe fheets, made of very fine linen, cofts from a hundred and fifty to a hundred and fixty livres of French money.

I purchafed at a table-cloth manufactory a dozen fmall napkins and a breakfaft-cloth. They were of an excellent quality, and coft me

me four Louis-d'or. I was happy to have an
opportunity of carrying them to France by
way of models.

I was alſo ſhewn, with an air of myſtery,
at the houſe of a rich manufacturer of fine
linen, an inſtrument as ingenious as uſeful for
aſcertaining the fineneſs of texture with the
greateſt preciſion.

It conſiſts of a kind of ſmall microſcope of
a very ſimple conſtruction, which, inſtead of
an object-glaſs, has a round hole, about three
lines or a little more in diameter. The glaſs
or lens correſponds to that circular aperture
at the diſtance of the focus. The inſtrument
is placed upon the cloth, the threads of which
are ſo magnified by the lens, that the obſerver
can eaſily count how many are contained
within the ſpace of the hole. It is evident
that the greater the number, the finer is the
fabric of the ſtuff. It likewiſe ſhews whether
the thread be too flat or otherwiſe. The
artiſan who is acquainted with the mode of
uſing the inſtrument, if he ſhould preſent a
piece of cloth which he charges as fine, has
no admiſſible excuſe when it is found to be of
a coarſer quality, by making himſelf count
the number of threads with this inſtrument.

The

The weavers, therefore, by its means, have become accustomed to the greatest precision.

The wholesale dealers equally employ it in their purchases. They have, therefore, good reason not to wish that every one should be acquainted with it; because, with its assistance, they can transact their business on a surer footing than those who are obliged to depend upon the naked eye. I brought one of these instruments to France, where they were soon multiplied.

VOLCANIC MOUNTAIN OF KINNOUL, IN THE VICINITY OF PERTH.

The desire of examining the hill of Kinnoul, was what principally determined me to pass through the town of Perth, from which it was only two miles and a quarter distant. I was therefore able to make several visits to it during the three days that I staid at Perth.

The lavas and agates which I collected there were very numerous. I spent half a day and a whole night in sorting and ticketing them. The number of the finest specimens were doubled, and in some cases tripled, for

the

the purpose of distributing them among my friends. The whole filled a large chest*.

Scarcely had I crossed the bridge of Perth, where I observed some lavas in strata, unformed masses, and ill-shaped prisms. These different currents proceeded from several eminences forming part of the mountain of Kinnoul, the basis of which, occupied a very considerable extent. Pursuing the road along the Tay, with the mountain on my left, for two miles and a quarter, I came to a very steep and almost perpendicular rock, nearly six hundred feet high, and on the very edge of the road. The traveller ought to make directly for this place, because it is the richest in agates and other productions worth collecting.

Though the mountain appears extremely steep in that quarter, one may, notwithstand-

---

* This chest, together with my whole collection of the products of Scotland and the Hebrides, which was in the best order, was lost on a sand bank, near Dunkirk. The vessel which carried them from Leith sunk, and only the crew were saved. By this unfortunate accident, I have lost all the fruits of a toilsome journey, except a small box of the most remarkable articles, which I brought along with me in my carriage. But I had carefully copied into one book the lists of all my collections.

ing,

ing, clamber up to its fummit, with a little precaution. But, for this purpofe, it is neceffary to have a ftout ftick, armed with an iron fpike; nor muft the adventurer hefitate to fcale the craggy rocks. This labour, however, may be faved by approaching in the direction juft mentioned, where the forms and different difpofitions of the ftrata are in a manner plainly legible in its fide, which is completely expofed to view. The following is a note of the different articles which I collected :—

VOLCANIC MINERALOGY OF KINNOUL.

1. Black bafaltes, of a fine grain and homogeneous texture, forming an extenfive current, adhering to a ftream of black porphyric lava, with a bafis of trapp, and fo difpofed as to leave no doubt that the bafaltic lava in this ftate derives its origin from porphyric lava. The latter has preferved its cryftals of felt fpar, which are fmall but well defined, whilft the bafaltic lava has loft its cryftals, which are amalgamated and blended with the very bafis of the porphyry, either by a fudden and violent, or a long-continued combuftion.

On

On examining the bafaltic lava with a microfcope, fmall cryftals are ftill feen in fome parts of it, which are not entirely amalgamated with the lava; their courfe may be pretty well traced, even from their exterior appearance. Small fplinters of the porphyric lava, on being urged with the blow-pipe, afford an enamel of a beautiful black colour; and the bafaltic lava yields a vitreous matter or enamel in every refpect fimilar.

2. The fame bafaltic lava, divided into large prifms, very irregular, though well defined. Thefe prifms prefent nothing in the fracture but an homogeneous lava, without the leaft cryftal of felt fpar.

3. Bafaltic lava of a delicate green colour, very hard, fometimes fonorous on being ftruck, difpofed in a large current. This greenifh lava tranfverfely interfects a current of black compact lava. Its greenifh colour is owing to a particular modification of iron. I was well acquainted with the earth of Verona, which has its origin from a very remarkable decompofition of a volcanic product; but I had never before feen a ftratum of compact, hard, and fonorous bafaltic lava, which had that greenifh appearance.

4. A qua-

4. A quadrangular prism, well defined, in excellent preservation, and of an agreeable delicate green colour. I found it among the wreck of a considerable mass of lava of the same colour, which had fallen from the top of the precipice.

5. The same greenish basaltic lava in a tabular form.

None of the green coloured lavas were magnetic.

6. Compact porphyric lava, of a black ground, studded with a number of crystals of white felt spar, which have not undergone any alteration. This lava is strongly magnetic.

7. A quadrangular prism of blackish porphyric lava, magnetic, with a knob of flesh-coloured agate on one of its faces.

8. Porphyric lava, mouldering into gravel, and forming extensive beds. I have no doubt that if this gravelly lava, which is not very hard, were reduced to powder by the aid of stamping-mills, like those used in Holland, for pounding the lavas or *tras* in the environs of Andernach, it would afford a puzzolano, an excellent cement, of great and indeed indispensable use for building in water.

9. Compact

9. Compact porphyric lava, with a ground of deep iron grey inclining to violet, intermixed with particles of green fteatites, fome knobs of variegated agate, and a few globules of white calcareous fpar, difpofed in a large current.

10. Compact porphyric lava, magnetic, with knobs of white, and fometimes flefh-coloured calcareous fpar, and globules of the fineft green-coloured fteatites.

11. Reddifh-coloured compact, porphyric lava, forming a layer between two currents of bafaltic lava of a delicate green colour, and adhering to them.

12. Black porphyric lava; magnetic, interfected with belts of red porphyric lava, refembling the red porphyry of the ancients. This lava, in which both the lavas are united, is very remarkable.

13. A geode of agate, internally ftudded with fhining cryftals of violet-coloured quartz, in the form of hexagonal pyramids, incrufted with compact porphyric lava, of a dark brown colour, a little inclining to violet, with fome knobs of white calcareous fpar, and feveral globules of agate and green fteatites.

14. A geode

14. A geode of bright red agate, having in its interior a brilliant cryftallization, of white quartz of the greateft purity. This geode is found in a black porphyric lava, which is magnetic.

15. Eye-fpotted agate of a delicate rofe colour, incrufted with dark brown compact porphyric lava, intermixed with globules of green fteatites. This fpecimen is very agreeable to the eye.

16. Red ftriped agate, inclofed in black porphyric lava, ftrongly magnetic.

17. Semi-tranfparent agate of the moft vivid red, in a porphyric lava inclining to violet, with knobs of white calcareous fpar, and globules of a delicate, green coloured fteatites.

18. A geode with a cruft of calcedonious blueifh occulated agate, internally ftudded with cryftals of fparkling quartz. In the interior of the cryftals are feen particles of black lava taken up during the procefs of cryftallization; from which it is beyond doubt that the formation of the geodes was pofterior to that of the lava.

19. A lump of white calcareous fpar, fparkling, difpofed in rhomboidal laminæ, amidft

amidft a flight envelope of fteatites of a fine green colour. The whole is incrufted in a black compact lava, magnetic, and more nearly refembling bafaltes than porphyry.

20. A lump of green fteatites, enveloped with a flight covering of white calcareous fpar, in a porphyric lava, of a brown colour, inclining to violet. This fragment is the reverfe of the preceding.

Such are the moft interefting articles which I collected on the mountain of Kinnoul. I have no doubt that a longer ftay would have confiderably augmented my collection. But others may perfect what I give here as a fketch only. I had neither direction nor guide to regulate my refearches on that mountain. It was not even fo much as conjectured to be volcanic at Perth. All that was known there refpecting it was, that fome Edinburgh lapidaries vifited it from time to time in queft of agates, which they polifhed and turned to an object of a petty traffic.

CHAP.

CHAPTER XII.

St. Andrews Univerſity.—Library.—Old Churches.— Natural Hiſtory.

WE ſet out from Perth for St. Andrews by way of the ſmall town of Cupar in Fife, where we changed horſes. We accompliſhed this journey in ſeven hours. All the hills on the road are formed of blackiſh gravelly lava and baſaltes.

We had letters of recommendation to Mr. George Hill, profeſſor of Greek, and Mr. Charles Wilſon, profeſſor of Hebrew, in the univerſity of St. Andrews. We waited upon theſe gentlemen on the following day, and both of them exerted themſelves with the greateſt eagerneſs to oblige us, and to procure us ſuch information as could gratify our taſte or curioſity.

UNIVERSITY.

This univerſity recommends itſelf to the notice of the traveller by the name of the celebrated Buchanan, who was profeſſor of philoſophy there.

There

There were formerly * two colleges which are now confolidated into one. There was a profeffor of the Latin language in each of the colleges; one of the profefforfhips is now fuppreffed, and a chair of Natural Hiftory fubftituted in its ftead. The Greek profeffor-fhip is alfo of recent erection.

The revenues of the profeffors, who are thirteen in number, amount together to fifteen hundred pounds fterling, which gives a fixed falary of nearly three thoufand French livres for each place.

The names of the profeffors are as follows:

Jofeph M'Cormick, Principal;
James Flint, profeffor of Medicine;
John Cook, Moral Philofophy;
George Forreft, Natural Philofophy;
Nicolas Vilant, Mathematics;
John Hunter, the Latin language;
George Hill, the Greek language;
W. Barron, Logic;
Hugh Cleghorn, Civil Hiftory;

* There were formerly three colleges, namely, St. Salvador's, St. Leonard's, and St. Mary's; the two former of which have been united. Tranflat.

Dr. J. Gillespie, } Divinity;
Dr. Henry Spence, }
William Brown, Church History;
Ch. Wilson, the Hebrew language.

LIBRARY.

The college library is open to the public for seven months in the year, during which they are at liberty to enter it every day at stated hours. There are likewise some other days of the year upon which it is opened. The revenues appropriated to the maintenance of this establishment arise from some tythes belonging to an old ecclesiastical foundation which were seized upon by the crown and afterwards assigned to this library. Their produce does not amount to more than thirty-six pounds sterling, a sum nowise adequate to the most urgent current expences. But some casual emoluments from the admission of graduates increases the total revenue of the library to the sum of an hundred and fifty pounds sterling. The number of books is not more than eleven or twelve thousand. They are almost all modern, with the exception of several bibles and some devotional books, among which there is nothing extraordinary.

I faw nothing worthy of notice but a manufcript which was fomewhat interefting from its excellent prefervation; it was a Saint Auguftin of the thirteenth century, written on vellum. There is alfo in the fame apartment, as an object of curiofity, an Egyptian mummy in a very bad ftate, without even its ancient cafe, and appearing to me to be one of thofe which the Arabians join together of patches and fragments for the purpofe of felling them to fuch as are unable to detect the impofition.

ANCIENT CATHOLIC CHURCHES.

This city, during the reign of the catholic religion, poffeffed the archiepifcopal pre-eminence. The famous Cardinal Beaton was one of its archbifhops. Vaft and fuperb churches announced the opulence of their founders, and the generous facrifices of a people powerfully attached to their mode of worfhip. The ruins of all thefe monuments, of which there are ftill fome fine remains, give the city an afpect of antiquity which forms a fingular contraft with the fimplicity, the modefty, and I had almoft faid, the poverty of the greater part of its prefent habitations.

The

The church of the second college, as it is called, which is still standing, appears to be very ancient. The steeple is a high tower, of a quadrangular form, and of a good and solid construction. The church is spacious, and in the gothic stile of building; it is consecrated to the Presbyterian worship, and contains the tomb, now partly in ruins, of an archbishop who founded the university of this city. This monument is built in the wall with stone of a very common kind, and exhibits nothing remarkable. On an occasion of making some repairs, there was discovered within it * a church mace, of gilt copper, four feet long. This ensign of dignity, which I was permitted to examine, is charged with gothic ornaments finely executed, but in a bad taste. It is covered with small steeples, and niches occupied by monks with cowls on their heads and in an attitude of prayer. The angles are filled with winged angels placed in pulpits and in a preaching

* The monument here referred to is the tomb of bishop Kennedy, within which were found six maces; three of them were distributed among the other Scotch universities, and the remaining three are preserved in that of St. Andrews. Translator.

posture.

posture. Gothic medallions are suspended all round it by way of ornament; and the whole is surmounted with a figure of Christ on foot, and standing upright in a pyramidal niche. This work, to judge by its stile, may be from two hundred and sixty to three hundred years old. It can only serve to give us an idea of the arts, and of the bad taste of the time.

We likewise visited another church, which, from an inscription on one of its doors, appeared to have been built in the year 1112. In this church we saw a grand mausoleum of white marble, representing an archbishop, as large as life, kneeling, and an angel placing a martyr's crown on his head. A spacious basso relievo, at the foot of this monument, exhibits the same archbishop attacked by some men who assassinate him. A young girl in tears, detained by some other persons, near a coach, which they have stopped, makes the most violent struggle to go to the assistance of the archbishop, in whom she seems to have the most tender interest. Despair is strongly marked in her gestures and her figure.

This scene instantly brought to my remembrance the disastrous event which happened

pened to Cardinal Beaton *, who was killed
on the 29th of May, 1546, by Norman Lefly,
eldeft fon of the earl of Rothes, accompanied
with fifteen confpirators. Beaton, was doubtlefs a man of great talents, but at the fame
time ambitious, infolent, a cruel enemy of
the Reformers, and had the abominable in-
humanity to caufe the unfortunate George
Wifhart to be burnt alive.

I was aftonifhed at feeing a monument of
this fort permitted to remain in a church now
applied to the ufe of the reformed religion,
which holds Beaton in fuch abhorrence. But
my aftonifhment foon ceafed on learning that
this monument, the fculpture of which was
executed in Holland, had been erected by the
relations of the archbifhop a long time after
his death, and that they had appropriated a
certain yearly fum for keeping it in repair.
It thence refults, that in order to obtain this
fum, the maufoleum muft be allowed to exift
as a work that has received their complete

* The author's conjecture has been in this inftance erroneous. This monument is a reprefentation of the death
of archbifhop Sharp, who, in revenge for his cruel perfecu-
tions of their fect, was affaffinated by nine prefbyterian
enthufiafts, on the 3d of May, 1669, on Magus Moor, in
the vicinity of St. Andrews.—Tranflator.

fanction. But it alfo happens that the monument receives no repairs, though it begins to be greatly in want of them; and the money is very probably applied to the ufe of the church. No part of it, however, will be demolifhed as long as the yearly allowance fhall continue to be paid: an evident proof that every where, and in every cafe, gold has the power of reconciling the moft oppofite opinions.

It would appear that the relations of cardinal Beaton had no wifh to conceal that the holy archbifhop was a father, fince his daughter is reprefented in tears, with her arms extended towards her father, and forcibly held by two of the confpirators, at the moment when the others accomplifh the murder. But the folemn Robertfon informs us, in his hiftory of Scotland, that the prelate openly acknowledged this daughter. "Cardinal Beaton," fays he, " with the fame " public pomp, which is due to a legitimate " child, celebrated the marriage of his natu- " ral daughter with the earl of Crawfurd's " fon;" and in a note he fays, " the marriage " articles, fubfcribed with his own hand, in " which he calls her *my daughter*, are
 " ftill

" ftill extant," vol. i. p. 88, of the 8vo. edition.

The facade of the church of St. Leonard, though gothic, poffeffes an elegance and grandeur which are very impreffive. This was the chapel of the college which has been diffolved. Johnfon in his *Journey to the Weftern Iflands of Scotland*, complains, that he was always by fome, civil excufe hindered from entering it, and that in fact it had been converted into a green-houfe. I was not more fortunate than Johnfon. But I found that the area in front and on one fide of the chapel was turned into a kitchen garden; and from what I faw myfelf, it is not improbable that the houfe of God has become the houfe of the gardener, and that it affords a fhelter to his carrots and his turnips during the winter.

By way of compenfation, however, I viewed at my eafe, the ruins of the cathedral and the adjoining palace, which formed the refidence of the archbifhop. Both thefe vaft edifices, flood on an elevated fituation, which commands a full profpect of the fea. The palace was, indeed, fo clofe to it, that the

waves

waves have undermined a part of its foundations.

The cathedral, as far as can be eſtimated from its remains, without compriſing ſome adjoining chapels, a kind of cloiſter, and other ſubordinate buildings around it, was three hundred and fifteen feet long, and ſixty feet broad. Nothing can be more remarkable and intereſting than this ruin. Not only does it bear the impreſſion of time and neglect, but it alſo diſcovers the ſtrongeſt marks of a religious and fanatical zeal which roſe to the moſt abominable phrenzy.

Towers of the moſt ſolid conſtruction overthrown; columns broken in pieces; the remains of magnificent gothic windows ſuſpended as it were in the air; pyramidal ſteeples, more than a hundred feet high, of ſtones ſo ſolidly laid, that it being difficult to demoliſh them entirely, they were pierced through and through and indented in every direction; winding ſtair-caſes which ſeem to ſtand without any foundation; altars heaped upon altars under the remaining vaults; fragments of friezes, capitals, entablatures, ſcattered among ſepulchral tablets, and mutilated tombs; the wreck of cloiſters, chapels, porticos;

ticos; and some columns still maintaining an erect posture in the midst of such wide-spread havock: such is a rapid sketch of the picture presented by these extensive ruins, which strike the man, who beholds them for the first time, with dread and astonishment.

The traveller is at first lost in conjecturing whether a terrible earthquake, a long siege, or an invasion of barbarians, was the cause of so much devastation. A quadrangular tower an hundred feet high, well constructed, and in perfect preservation, rises single and unimpaired by the side of these vast ruins. It is difficult to account for this contrast.

At the view of this scene one is irresistibly led into a train of melancholy reflexions, on the maladies of the mind, which degenerate into madness and mortify our reason. Are these frenzies, these deliriums of the intellect, like corporeal diseases, inseparable from the condition of humanity? If the affirmative be true, mankind in the gross, are the most ferocious, and at the same time the most mischievous of animals, and one might be tempted to renounce this life at once, were it not for a few chosen individuals who encourage one to support it.

I was

I was affured that the quadrangular tower which ftands entire in the midft of thefe extenfive ruins, has exifted for upwards of eleven hundred years. It was probably a light-houfe in former times; at prefent it is a memorial only of the feudal rights which the king has over the city; and on this account it is preferved with great care. I mounted by an infide ftair-cafe to the higheft balcony; whence there is a view of a wide extent of country.

Blaauve has inferted in his large atlas very exact engravings of the principal monuments of St. Andrews, as they appeared at an epoch when they exifted in all their fplendour. Mr. Cleghorn affured me, that the materials which had been furnifhed to Blaauve were very correct.

Thefe fame monuments, in their ruinous ftate, have been carefully engraved in four plates, by Pouncy, from drawings of ftriking effect, by J. Oliphant. I faw a collection of them at the houfe of the college librarian, who would not agree to fell them for any money. He carefully preferved them in frames of glafs; he faid they were now very fcarce, and hardly to be met with for fale.

Before

Before a crowd of fanatics, inflamed to fury by the homicidal fermons of the gloomy Knox, carried the torch of deftruction to men and things, through that unfortunate city, it was a place of confiderable eminence ; letters and the fciences flourifhed within its walls, and rich and numerous eftablifhments were dedicated to public inftruction.

The blow which it received from the hand of barbarians, fuddenly changed its appearance. It requires ages to build, but an inftant only to deftroy. This city, notwithftanding the length of time which has elapfed fince the date of its misfortunes, ftill appears as if it had been ravaged by the peftilence. Its ftreets are large and commodious ; but are every where covered with grafs. All is fadnefs and filence. Its inhabitants, ignorant of commerce and the arts, prefent only the image of indolence and languor. This ftate of inactivity has its correfpondent effects on the population ; for though the place is ftill capable of lodging from fourteen to fifteen thoufand people, it does not contain at moft above three thoufand.

I therefore join in the opinion of Johnfon, who, indignant at the defolate condition in which

which the English government suffers establishments consecrated to instruction to remain, exclaims, " It is surely not without " just reproach that a nation, of which the " commerce is hourly extending, and the " wealth increasing, denies any participation " of its prosperity to its literary societies; " and while its merchants or its nobles are " raising palaces, suffers its universities to " moulder into dust."

SOME OBJECTS OF NATURAL HISTORY IN THE ENVIRONS OF ST. ANDREWS.

The rock on which the castle of this city stood, is in many places at least one hundred feet above the level of the sea; and the place itself, though built on a plain, has the same height above the water.

This huge precipice consists of beds of white quartzose free-stone, crossed at intervals with small horizontal layers of black argillaceous schistus, soft, a little shining, and deriving its colour from impalpable particles of pit-coal.

In the part where the free-stone comes in contact with the schistus, the first is always
divided

divided into small strata which easily separate, and are themselves somewhat tinged with coaly particles. There also may be distinguished some small bits of wood converted into coal.

To these alternate beds of free-stone, coloured with coal, and of black argillaceous schistus, succeed thick banks of white freestone, interrupted in their turn with thin layers of black schistus and coloured free-stone; but here the coaly particles are more copious.

In short, under the deepest beds of freestone in the part where the sea has uncovered them, are seen strata of coal almost pure and fit for burning.

Industry is here in such a state of stagnation that no person has attempted, by following these remarkable indications, to sink a pit, or even so much as to found for a mine of coals which presents itself under such favourable appearances, and which from its situation on the very edge of the sea, would form a source of riches to the country.

I expressed my astonishment on the subject to several intelligent persons, who framed excuses for this negligence, by saying, that three or four miles inland there were some mines

of

of coal worked, which were fufficient for the fupply of the country.

The fea, notwithftanding the barriers oppofed to it by the bold bank of free-ftone on which St. Andrews is built, has gained upon the land fo perceptibly, that, as I was affured on the ftrongeft authority, within lefs than two hundred and fifty years, it had undermined and worn the rock with fuch activity as to deftroy almoft the whole of the fcite of the ancient archiepifcopal caftle. A road which led from the caftle to a mole ftill exifting is entirely carried away, fo that the water completely intercepts the paffage in a direct line; and it fhould be remarked, that the fpace deftroyed between the caftle and the head of the mole is about five hundred toifes. Thus has the fea in fo fhort a period wafted away a very confiderable extent and thicknefs of folid rock; and at low water nothing is to be feen but rubbifh and ruins.

From this encroachment, however, we are not to form general conclufions refpecting the advancing or receding of the waters of the ocean. It is a circumftance purely local that has occafioned this accidental invafion, which
I regard

I regard as completely unconnected with any general theory.

By an attentive examination of the spot, I difcovered fome of the caufes of this great degradation.

And firft, the facility which there has always been of drawing large maffes of free-ftone from this craggy tract on the reflux of the tide, is one caufe, which we will not be apt to reject, if we confider that the immenfe quantity of materials employed in conftructing the cathedral, feveral large churches and convents, the caftle and the houfes of the city, has been taken out of this place. I myfelf faw a great number of workmen employed in cutting out pretty large ftones for fome repairs which were making on the mole.

On the other hand, the pofition of the beds, the various fubftances of which they are compofed, and their unequal degrees of hardnefs, tend to accelerate their degradation. The coaft is fo fteep that the deep excavation which extends from the caftle to the mole-head, bears the name of *the Precipice.*

The maffes of free-ftone being placed on beds of argillaceous fchiftus, which is foft, pyritous

pyritous and fusceptible of being dissolved by water, are liable to slide from their place and to lose their balance. The upper beds give a violent concussion to the others in their fall; and this permant cause of destruction, joined to the action of frost, the atmosphere, and the changes of wet and dryness, must at length occasion extensive havock. But what is very remarkable and worthy of attention, is, that all these fragments, which are subject to the powerful action of the waves and currents of the sea, being dashed against each other or rolled upon the hard and rugged bottom, are soon reduced to powder; thence there result considerable deposites of sand which the sea throws up in banks on the beach, and which the winds form into small hills. Thus the waves which tear asunder the free-stone and carry it off the coast in huge solid pieces, throw it back on a neighbouring part in the form of sand, which may in time acquire consistence and form good soil.

It is easy to perceive the identity of this sand, which is intermixed with some coal and clayey matter, with the free-stone, whence it originated. This newly formed tract of sand occupies a space of four miles long, and half

a mile

a mile broad *. Such is probably the origin of the greater part of fands, which may in a courfe of time, and with the aid of certain circumftances, be a fecond time formed into free-ftone.

I ought to have ftated, before difmiffing the fubject of *the Precipice*, that the inferior ftrata, which fupport a mafs more than eighty feet thick of fchiftus and free-ftone, are themfelves very remarkable, being compofed of very hard free-ftone, and containing pebbles of different forms and fizes, and of a reddifh colour in their cruft or exterior furface. On breaking thefe pebbles, they are eafily difcovered to confift of black bafaltic lava, ftill retaining their magnetic quality, though their cruft has undergone alteration.

As the rounded lavas thus confined are feen in great number in the lower beds of free-ftone, and as it is probable that thofe which have been invaded by the fea contained fimilar ones, it is beyond doubt that thefe pebbles exifted prior to the formation of the

---

* In thefe fands are found feveral living fhell-fifh. The large razor fifh or *follen*, the *cardium fenatum* of Linnæus, or *bucarde dentè* of Bruguiere, defcribed in his article on the Natural Hiftory of Worms, page 227, of the French Encyclopædia, and the *cardium ciliare* of Linnæus, or *bucarde frange* of Bruguiere, page 218 of the fame book, are very common.

free-ſtone; that is to ſay, that they are the products of volcanos, and that they have been rounded by the ſea before the ſandy ſubſtances became united and conſolidated into a maſs of free-ſtone.

There is no room for any doubt or heſitation reſpecting the quality of the ſubſtances. The baſaltic pebbles are ſo many traces of diſcovery and uſeful indications to thoſe who endeavour to peruſe the grand volume of nature. But this is not a fit place to expatiate further upon the ſubject. I ſhall only ſay, that if accidental circumſtances of this kind cannot determine to a very nigh degree the time which has elapſed ſince the formation of theſe lavas and the free-ſtone, in which they are incloſed, they induce us at leaſt to believe that both the one and the other muſt have taken place at a very remote epoch.

CHAP-

CHAPTER XIII.

Departure from St. Andrews.—Largo.—Leven.— Dyfart—Kirkaldy.—Kinghorn.—Leith. — Return to Edinburgh.

SCARCELY had we left St. Andrews and entered on the road to Largo, when we found the fields fcattered over with very large blocks of bafaltes. The farmers have inclofed their lands with them, and thus afforded to naturalifts an eafy opportunity of examining them.

They are of a fine black colour, great hardnefs, and a pure and homogeneous fubftance. I attentively examined a great number of the ftones which were but recently broken, to try whether any extraneous body had entered into their internal compofition. But I found their texture in general very pure, and found in a fingle lump only a few fmall cryftals of black fchorl. The fchorls are in general very rarely met with in the volcanic produéts of Scotland and the Hebrides.

After a ride of three miles, we reached a pretty high flat, entirely covered with blocks of of bafaltes, which feemed to have been fcattered about at random, and which very much incommode cultivation, as it would not be an eafy matter to difplace them. This elevated plain is of vaft extent, and yields oats and rye; though the vegetable mould cannot be much more than five or fix inches in depth.

This cultivated foil repofes on blackifh argillaceous fchiftus, difpofed in ftrata. Banks of free-ftone, like thofe of St. Andrews, fucceed the fchiftus, and then follow at a confiderable depth beds of excellent coal. The number of pits which are feen along the road, announce that the collieries are worked with great activity. I counted more than fifteen coal-pits within the fpace of a mile.

Largo is only a fmall village; we ftopped at it to bait our horfes. Banks of free-ftone of great thicknefs are expofed to view on all fides; they are over-topped with enormous pieces of bafaltes. I had not before feen in the volcanic parts of Scotland, detached maffes of bafaltes of fo great a bulk. This compact lava is very pure and found, fo that it may be formed into flabs or even ftatues.

Leven and Dyfart are pretty large villages, which lie on the road by the fea-fide. In
their

their environs are feveral collieries, which employ a great number of perfons. They are carried on upon a greater fcale than thofe in the neighbourhood of St. Andrews, and conducted with greater intelligence and more extenfive means. Thofe of the inhabitants who are not employed in the collieries apply themfelves to fifhing, in which they are very fkilful.

Kirkaldy is a confiderable burgh. The whole of its environs is ftrewed with blocks of bafaltes; and this fcattered train of lavas extends from Largo to beyond Kirkaldy, along a fpace of more than twenty-four miles in length, and eight miles in breadth. What terrible convulfion was it that tranfported thefe bafaltes, and thus rolled and difperfed them over fo vaft a furface?

I had already feen in Vivarais, a ftate of things in every refpect fimilar; but upon a plain much higher above the coaft of Maire. The maffes of bafaltes are there equally large and not lefs numerous. They may be traced to the fmall town of Pradelle, through an extent of more than twenty miles long, and four or five miles broad. This refemblance ought not to efcape confideration.

From

From Kirkaldy we purfued our road to Kinghorn, a burgh fituated on the water's edge. The blocks of bafaltes feemed to multiply as we approached the vicinity of Kinghorn; but very near the town we found the bafaltes in imbodied maffes, that is, difpofed in large currents as it was difcharged by the volcanos.

Between Kirkaldy and Kinghorn, and at a little diftance from the road, are three upright rude ftones, which have been erected as a memorial of fome event, which it is now impoffible to trace. Thefe monuments confift of a rough-grained yellowifh free-ftone. The higheft is about fifteen feet above ground, and muft have funk at leaft five feet below the furface; it is of confiderable thicknefs: the other two are not fo large. They appear to be of very high antiquity. Have they been erected by the Romans? This is not very probable; for, that warlike people, at the time they over-ran England and attempted to fubjugate the Caledonians, who gave them the moft vigorous refiftance, were too familiar with the arts, to raife fuch ruftic monuments which have no infcription, nor any mark of workmanfhip. It is not improbable

probable that thefe rude columns were con-
fecrated to the fuperftition of the ancient
Druids, or that they were erected by a warlike people little fkilled in the arts, in
remembrance of fome important events
which have not defcended to our knowledge.

Monuments of this kind are very numerous in Scotland and the Hebrides. The
natives entertain various and doubtful opinions upon the fubject. Some call them
the altars, temples, or monuments of the
Druids; while others, regarding them as of
greater antiquity, fay, that they were erected
in the time of Fingal; that is, at an epoch
indeterminate, and perhaps fabulous; and
another clafs maintain that they are Roman
tombs, and contain the afhes of illuftrious
warriors, who fell in their combats with the
Caledonians. I fhall leave the developement
of this enigma to the Edinburgh Antiquarian Society, with merely calling to their
recollection that fimilar monuments are
found in Lower Brittany, and that the language of its inhabitants has a ftrong refemblance to that of the Hebridians, and I entertain the hope that they will throw fome
light

light upon a subject so worthy of being investigated.

There are twenty-seven miles from St. Andrews to Kinghorn. We were obliged to use the same horses for the whole way; there being no place where we could change them. Kinghorn is situated on the edge of the sea; and at this place is the ferry for crossing the Frith of Forth to Leith, which is within a very short distance of Edinburgh.

The beach of Kinghorn, and, indeed, of the whole coast, is bordered with layers of lava; some of them in the form of basaltes, in an extended mass, or in prisms, and others in a gravelly and decomposed state. These several streams of volcanic matter repose immediately on an argillaceous schistus under which are frequently found beds of coals.

In the lavas of Kinghorn I found some zeolite, and a great deal of calcareous spar, adhering to decomposed lavas.

The passage from Kinghorn to the port of Leith is seven miles. We performed it in two hours, in one of the ferry-boats, which are tolerably commodious, and set out regularly at certain hours. In the middle of the

Frith is a very rapid current, which is obfervable at all times; for, where it runs, the fea is always agitated during the greateft calms.

The harbour of Leith, at the time we entered it, was filled with veffels, Englifh, Scotch, American, &c. I faw feveral veffels belonging to Glafgow and Leith, which were done over with bitumen or tar, extracted from pit-coal at the manufactures of Lord Dundonald, who has introduced the making and ufing of this tar on a great fcale in that country. The veffels coated with it appeared of a fine fhining black, which diftinguifhed them from the others. Several fhip-mafters whom I fpoke to on the fubject, and fome of whom had come from the Weft Indies, affured me that their veffels which had been covered with this tar, arrived in the beft poffible condition, and were completely free from worm-holes. Navigation is doubtlefs much indebted to Lord Dundonald, who perfevered with the moft undeviating conftancy, in bringing to perfection this ufeful product of coal, and alfo in bringing it into general ufe, a thing not eafily effected upon every occafion when it is neceffary to change ancient cuftoms.

We

We reached the harbour of Leith about fix in the afternoon of the 16th of October. William Thornton, who proceeded directly forward from Perth, without accompanying us to St. Andrews, waited for us at Edinburgh. We went from Leith to Edinburgh in lefs than half an hour, along a fuperb road.

Thornton had procured us lodgings at a private houfe, and at a reafonable rate; for we had determined not to go to Dun's Hotel, where fuch exactions had been practifed on us during our firft ftay in that city. Our new lodgings, for ourfelves and our three domeftics, coft only eighty-four livres a week.

As we intended to fpend a fortnight at Edinburgh, we made an arrangement with the mafter of a tavern who ferved us with provifions, dreffed in the French ftile, adding a few Scotch difhes, which were agreeable to us. This man is a native of Bourdeaux, and was brought from France by a Scotch Lord, with whom he refided a long time. He afterwards married and fettled in Edinburgh. He is a very good landlord and full of attention and complaifance. I would recommend his houfe to fuch naturalifts and

others

others as intend to vifit Edinburgh. They have only to afk for the mafter of the French tavern, which is very well known.

At this table, we formed an acquaintance with Baron Hartfield, whofe ordinary refidence is at Berlin. He is a man of eftimation and talent, and travelled for the purpofes of information. He had pufhed his refearches as far as the Hebrides, and vifited the ifle of Staffa; in his paffage to which, he told us, he encountered the moft imminent danger.

CHAPTER XIV.

Edinburgh.—The Univerſity.—Learned Societies.— College of Phyſicians.—College of Surgeons.—Cabinet of Natural Hiſtory.—Robertſon.—Smith.— Black.—Cullen, &c.

EDINBURGH is ſituated in 55° 57′ of north latitude, and 3° 14′ of weſt longitude, from the meridian of Greenwich. The diſtance of this city from London is, by the eaſt road, through Berwick, 388 miles; by the middle road, through Wooler, 378 miles; and by the weſt road, through Carliſle, 396 miles.

The ſciences, literature, natural hiſtory, and the arts, being the principal objects of my journey; what I ſhall have to ſay of Edinburgh will chiefly relate to them: topographical deſcriptions of this city are to be found in a number of other works.

THE UNIVERSITY.

The following is the eſtabliſhment of the Univerſity of Edinburgh, with the names of thoſe who were at this time its profeſſors.

The

The King, is the Protector;
Doctor Robertſon, Principal;
Robert Hamilton and A. Hunter, pro-
feſſors of Theology;
Robert Cumming, Church Hiſtory;
Doctor J. Robertſon, Hebrew;
A. Dalziel, Greek;
D. Stewart, Mathematics;
A. Ferguſſon, Moral Philoſophy;
J. Robiſon, Natural Philoſophy;
A. Tytler and J. Pringle, Civil Hiſtory;
William Wallace, Scottiſh Law;
Robert Dick, Civil Law;
A. M'Conochie, the Law of Nature and
Nations;
Hugh Blair, Rhetoric;
John Hope, Botany;
Francis Home, Materia Medica;
William Cullen, Practice of Medicine;
James Gregory, Theory of Medicine;
Joſeph Black, Chymiſtry;
Alexander Monro, Anatomy;
Alexander Hamilton, Midwifery;
John Walker, Natural Hiſtory.

ROYAL SOCIETY.

The Duke of Buccleugh is Preſident of the
Royal Society;
Henry Dundas, Vice-Preſident.

The

The Prefidents of the Phyfical and Literary
Claffes, &c. are

Baron Gordon;
Lord Elliock;
General H. Campbel;
Adam Smith;
John M'Laurin;
Doctor Adam Ferguffon;
Doctor Monro;
Doctor Hope;
Doctor Black;
Doctor Hutton;
Profeffor Dugald Stewart;
John Playfair;
Profeffor J. Robertfon, Secretary.

ANTIQUARIAN SOCIETY—COLLEGE OF PHY-
SICIANS—COLLEGE OF SURGEONS—MEDI-
CAL SOCIETY.

There is a fociety lately eftablifhed in this city for the purpofe of collecting and preferving every thing that relates to Scottifh antiquities. The Earl of Bute is the Prefident, the Earl of Buchan is Firft Vice-Prefident, and Lord Gardenftone is Second Vice-Prefident.

There are befides a college of phyficians, a college of furgeons, and a medical fociety.

There is alfo a popular eftablifhment called the *High School of the City*, which announces that here nothing connected with public inftruction is neglected. This fchool is divided into feveral claffes, the mafters of which are employed in teaching the elements of the Latin language to youth.

Thefe inftitutions fhew that the arts, the fciences, and the Belles-lettres are cultivated and efteemed in this city, which is honoured by the diftinguifhed characters it has produced in every branch of learning. The celebrity of the profeffors is fo great that vaft numbers of foreigners come from every quarter of the world to ftudy at the univerfity, and the money they fpend is a confiderable advantage to the town.

Edinburgh, both from its fituation and its tranquillity, is a proper place for the fciences. It is not difturbed by the tumult of parliamentary difcuffions, the buftle of an overgrown commerce, nor the diftracting amufements of London. From time immemorial the mufes have chofen to refide on the top of a hill near a folitary fountain.

Mentioning the mufes, brings to my recollection an infcription in their honour, which is placed above one of the gates of the univerfity. It is rather extraordinary:

MUSIS ET CHRISTO.

TO THE MUSES AND CHRIST.

This affociation may to fome appear profane, but it is only a little conceit by which the author probably intended to announce that both letters and religion are taught in this building. A minifter of the prefbyterian religion, who accompanied me on my vifit to the univerfity, was very eager to juftify this fingular infcription, which he thought remarkably ingenious: He afked my opinion of it.

I replied to him with a fmile, that I believed the infcription might be interpreted in a very favourable manner, if the meaning which I was inclined to give it, were adopted.

It is proper, faid I, that the mufes fhould prefide over an eftablifhment which elevates man to the true dignity of his nature by inftructing him. They may be here confidered

as

as supplicating reason to proscribe the two chairs of *Theology* and *Church History;* and of those of *Logic, Moral Philosophy, Natural Philosophy, the Laws of Nature and Nations, Civil Law,* and *Scotch Law,* to make only one, which may be called the Professorship of the *Laws of Nature and Nations.*

On the other hand, the greatest of moralists, placed by the side of the muses, ought to remind the inhabitants of these countries that true knowledge is the enemy of fanaticism and intolerance; that those who have shed so much of the blood of Scotland in theological disputes, were strangers to morality as well as to the spirit of humanity, which belongs to the religion they pretended to profess *; and that those who overthrew and destroyed the ancient monuments of the nation, because they were connected with a religion which they did not approve, were real barbarians, whose ferocity was only equalled by their ignorance.

* Such as Knox, who entitled an account of the assassination of Cardinal Beaton, " The Joyous Narration, " &c." Such as that sanguinary priest, Beaton himself, who burnt human beings alive, because they were what he called heretics.

CABINET OF NATURAL HISTORY.

The cabinet of natural hiftory, in the univerfity, is under the direction of Doctor Howard. The examination of this collection gave me great pleafure, and interefted me much more than that of the Britifh Mufeum, in London, though it was far lefs confiderable; but, the objects which compofe it, are in a more methodical order, particularly the ftones and minerals: Befides, the managers of this mufeum have very properly taken care to collect all the productions of Scotland they have been able to procure.

Thus this mufeum is as inftructive and interefting to the natives of Scotland, as it is agreeable to foreigners, who are always much more defirous of feeing collections of the natural and local riches of a country, than the multitude of difconnected and inconfequential objects conftantly brought from India, and which are repeated over and over in every cabinet.

Some reforms are, however, wanting to the mufeum of the univerfity. The place allotted for it ought to be larger and decorated

rated with more tafte. The claffification fhould alfo be extended to the other parts as well as the minerals. Thefe improvements will certainly one day take place; that they have not been made already can only be afcribed to the remaining influence of that erroneous mode of education which in all ancient univerfities has occafioned natural fcience to be too much neglected. It is only lately that a profefforfhip in this important branch of inftruction was eftablifhed in the college of Edinburgh; but as a tafte for this delightful ftudy will, doubtlefs, increafe very rapidly in a city where the other fciences have fo long fixed their refidence, it is to be hoped that this cabinet will foon be placed in a building more worthy of a nation which is capable of furnifhing it with the richeft fpecimens. I therefore invite Doctor Howard, who poffeffes much knowledge, and who loves his country, to folicit from the government the grant of a building fuitable to the collection he fuperintends, with grounds fufficiently extenfive to join the botanical garden to the cabinet of natural hiftory.

Lithology, and the ftudy of minerals, have as yet made little progrefs in Scotland. There are

are therefore few collections of these objects. Doctor James Hutton is, perhaps, the only individual in Edinburgh who has placed in his cabinet some minerals and a number of agates chiefly found in Scotland; but I observed, that he had not been sufficiently careful in collecting the different matrices which contained them. I therefore experienced much more pleasure in conversing with this modest philosopher than in examining his collection, which presented me with nothing new, since I had seen and studied upon a large scale and in the places where nature had deposited them, almost all the specimens of his collection.

Doctor Hutton was at this time busily employed in writing a work on the theory of the earth *.

* This work, which contains rather general views of the subject than a body of observations, appeared in 1785, in the translations of the Royal Society of Edinburgh, for that year, under the following title: "Theory of the Earth, " or an Investigation of the Laws observable in the com- " position, dissolution, and restoration of land upon the " globe, by James Hutton, M.D. F.R.S.E. and Member " of the Royal Academy of Agriculture at Paris *."

* This work has since been considerably enlarged; in 1795, it was published in 2 vols. 8vo. under this title, *Theory of the Earth, with Proofs and Illustrations, in four parts.*—Translator.

During

During my refidence at Edinburgh I vifited, as often as poffible, the celebrated chymift, Dr. Black, who in 1761 gave the firft analyfis of calcareous earth, in which he demonftrated the exiftence of the aerial acid, commonly called fixed air. This illuftrious philofopher honoured me with the moft polite and kind attention.

After dining with him one day he fhewed me two pieces of petrified, or more properly, *quartzified* wood; for, upon examining them with a microfcope, it appeared that the quartzofe juice had penetrated through all their parts, and given them fuch a degree of hardnefs that they ftruck fire with fteel. This wood had been fent to Doctor Black from Ireland. Their colour was brown, and nearly the fame as that of the wood of Mahalep when it is worked.

This wood penetrated by quartz in the manner I have defcribed, poffeffes the following fingular property: If fmall fragments are broken off with a hammer and thrown on a piece of burning coal, in about a minute an agreeable fmell is perceived refembling that which proceeds from the wood of aloes.

It is doubtlefs aftonifhing that the effential odoriferous oil of this wood fhould have been preferved during the long time neceffary for transforming the wood into a ftate of quartzofe petrifaction; but fuppofing that fome particular circumftances had accelerated the petrification, it is ftill very extraordinary that this wood, which bears all the marks of a vegetable foreign to thefe countries, fhould be found on the banks of Lough Neigh in Ireland.

Doctor Black was pleafed to give me the two fpecimens he had of this curious wood, informing me at the fame time, that he did not collect objects of this kind, and that he fhould be very happy if I would place them in my cabinet.

This learned chymift alfo fhewed me the mechanifm of a portable furnace of his own invention, which will prove of great utility in the arts, and in chymiftry. It is fo contrived that the heat may not only be gradually increafed at pleafure, but carried to fuch a high degree as to reduce iron nails to a ftate of fufion. This plan may be extended and perhaps even applied to high furnaces in which iron ore is fmelted.

I fhall

I shall describe the manner in which the interior of this furnace is formed: for in it the merit of the invention chiefly consists. It is made of thick iron plates, and differs very little in its structure from the ordinary stove. Its form is cylindrical, and a cover is fitted to the top, which is occasionally taken off to supply the stove with fuel.

The mode by which the air enters is through holes of different sizes formed in a ring which turns round, so as to give facility to the admission of the air in the quantity wanted: but I repeat it, the construction is not the great merit of the invention, for I have seen, both in France and Germany, many furnaces, the mechanism of which is nearly the same with this, as well with respect to the mode of graduating the admission of the air as that of raising the heat to the degree required.

It is the manner in which the interior is covered, and the substances used for fuel that do honour to the profound knowledge of Doctor Black.

A quantity of the best charcoal is reduced to a fine powder, and passed through a sieve; some fine clay is also reduced to powder: the

colour

colour of the latter is of no importance; the leaſt fuſible and the moſt refractible, is the beſt.

The clay is ſoaked in water in a tray, in the proportion of a quart to three quarts of charcoal duſt. This mixture is well kneaded and amalgamated, and the paſte which is formed, is left in a ſtate of moiſture. If the clay be very glutinous, the proportion of charcoal is encreaſed. The inſide of the furnace is then plaſtered over with a quantity of this compoſition ſufficient to form a thin bed, which is ſmoothed with the hand and rendered every where as equal as poſſible. This firſt plaſter is made about a line thick, and allowed to dry ſlowly, without the operation of fire, that it may not be expoſed to the danger of cracking. When this firſt plaſter has acquired a ſufficient degree of hardneſs, a ſecond bed is formed; which being allowed to dry, a third is laid over it in the ſame manner. Thus different beds are formed in ſucceſſion above each other until the plaſter has acquired the thickneſs of about an inch.

Great attention muſt be paid to drying the beds ſlowly and forming them into one body, to which the fire will afterwards give great conſiſtence.

It

It is well known to experimental philofophers and chymifts, that charcoal is one of the worft conductors of heat. Founders, blackfmiths, and other workmen, have long been acquainted with this fact, tranfmitted from father to fon, and have ufed charcoal duft to great advantage in many of their operations without thinking of the manner in which it acted. The ufeful effects it produces are, however, refult lefs from its combuftible quality than that of its being a bad conductor of heat; or rather that it retains the heat, concentrates it, and prevents it from efcaping and lofing itfelf on the furrounding points.

I have been induced to enter into thefe details, becaufe I am of opinion that what has been faid will not prove inufeful to the arts, and that thofe who love and cultivate this particular branch of economy, may make fuccefsful applications of Doctor Black's invention. Thefe motives will excufe the length of this article.

I was feveral times in company with Doctor John Aiken, a private profeffor of Anatomy, in Edinburgh. He fhewed me a number of ingenious machines of his invention;

tion; and, among others, one for facilitating difficult births, the ufe of which was not at all dangerous, and in the invention of which he had followed nature as clofely as poffible.

This inftrument may be compared to a long flender hand. It is introduced quite open and without any kind of compreffion into the womb of the mother. This artificial hand, which is covered with a fine foft fkin, is placed againft the child upon which it is made to collapfe to the degree of contraction wanted, by the means of a fcrew in the handle, which acts with a gradual and gentle motion. The accoucheur then ufing his right hand, aided by this point of fupport, may deliver a woman in difficult labour with much more facility than in any other manner. Doctor Aikin affured me, that he had experienced the greateft fuccefs in the ufe of this inftrument.

The knowledge of whatever may contribute to relieve fuffering humanity, ought to be as widely diffufed as poffible. I therefore begged Doctor Aiken to allow me to take a model of this inftrument to France. He readily confented, and procured an excellent workman, who in a few days executed an
inftru-

inftrument perfectly fimilar. I packed it up with the intention of bringing it to Paris, and fubmitting it to the examination of our moft celebrated practitioners in midwifery.

Doctor Aiken alfo fhewed me a lock which he had contrived for great guns, by which they might be eafily made to perform a double difcharge; but while I admired his inventive genius, I could not avoid telling him, that I was far better pleafed to fee fo fkilful a phyfician employed in healing than in deftroying, and that I loved his invention for bringing men into the world, much more than I did that for fending them out of it.

Some days after, I had the pleafure of dining with Doctor Cullen, who, perhaps, is the oldeft, and certainly is one of the moft celebrated phyficians of Europe. The fcience of medicine owes him great obligations, and the city of Edinburgh ought never to forget that his reputation has attracted within its walls a multitude of foreigners who come from all quarters of the world to receive inftruction in that learned fchool, in the creation of which he has had a principal fhare.

Doctor

Doctor Cullen lived in the midſt of a numerous family, who formed around him an amiable circle of friends. Good nature and amenity reigned in his houſe. This learned phyſician merited all theſe advantages, for he poſſeſſed himſelf manners and a diſpoſition of the moſt agreeable kind. I found that he very much reſembled Bouffon in his behaviour and mode of living, which rendered him doubly intereſting to me. His table was plentifully ſerved, but without any luxury. I was however aſtoniſhed to find a profuſion of punch brought in between the deſert and tea.

This regimen, in the houſe of a phyſician of ſuch great reputation, appeared to me very extraordinary. He obſerved my ſurpriſe, and ſaid to me with a ſmile, that this beverage was not only ſuited to his age, but that a long experience had convinced him that when taken with moderation it was very ſalutary for the inhabitants of Scotland, particularly during the latter part of the autumnal ſeaſon, and in winter, becauſe the cold humidity which then prevails in this climate often checks perſpiration. *Punch*, he remarked, *is a warm ſtimulant, which operates wonderfully in main-*

maintaining that neceſſary ſecretion, or in reſtoring it to its equilibrium.

This humid and penetrating atmoſphere had, for ſome time, affected me in a very diſagreeable manner notwithſtanding the active life which I led. I am perſuaded, that it is one of the cauſes of that ſombre melancholy to which the people of England are ſo frequently liable. In vain I took exerciſe, and endeavoured to employ my time in a manner perfectly ſuitable to my taſte; I found that the miſts, the frequent rains, the daily winds, paſſing ſuddenly from heat to cold, a ſharpneſs in the air, which cannot be ſo eaſily deſcribed as it is felt; the abſence of the ſun, which fogs or clouds almoſt conſtantly eclipſe at this ſeaſon, plunged me into an involuntary melancholy, which I ſhould not have been able to ſupport long.

To raiſe my ſpirits, my friends often informed me that the ſun was about to appear; but in my bad humour, I was more than once tempted to reply to them, as Caraccioli, the viceroy of Sicily did to an Engliſh nobleman, who deſired him to look at that luminary in London: " Your Engliſh ſun, my lord, " very much reſembles our Sicilian moon."

This

This difagreeable feeling was not to be endured, and I refolved to adopt the regimen of Doctor Cullen. Each day after dinner I took a glafs of punch, compofed of rum, fugar, lemon juice, a little nutmeg and boiling water, which foon reftored me to my ufual condition *.

I faw feveral other men diftinguifhed in various branches of literature, among whom were Doctor Anderfon, Sir John Dalrymple, and the celebrated hiftorian Doctor William Robertfon, with whom I enjoyed many agreeable converfations.

That venerable philofopher, Adam Smith, was one of thofe whom I vifited moft frequently. He received me on every occafion in the kindeft manner, and ftudied to procure for me every information and amufement that Edinburgh could afford.

Smith had travelled in France, and refided for fome time in Paris. His collection of books was numerous and excellently chofen: The beft French authors occupied a diftin-

---

* That excellent phyfician, Doctor Cullen, is no more. He was regretted by his friends, and mourned by the city of Edinburgh which erected a funeral monument to his memory: He was worthy of that honour, and that city was worthy of him.

guished place in his library, for he was very fond of our language.

Though advanced in years he still possessed a fine figure. The animation of his countenance was striking, when he spoke of Voltaire, whom he had known and whose memory he revered, " Reason," said he, one day, as he shewed me a fine bust of this author, " owes him incalculable obligations;
" the ridicule and the sarcasms which he so
" plentifully bestowed upon fanatics and
" hypocrites of all sects, have enabled the
" understandings of men to bear the light of
" truth, and prepared them for those enquiries
" to which every intelligent mind ought to
" aspire. He has done much more for the
" benefit of mankind than those grave philo-
" sophers whose books are read by a few
" only; the writings of Voltaire are made
" for all and read by all."

On another occasion he observed to me,
" I cannot pardon the emperor Joseph II.
" who pretended to travel as a philosopher,
" for passing Ferney without paying homage
" to the historian of the Czar Peter I. From
" this circumstance I concluded that Joseph
" was but a man of inferior mind."

One evening while I was at tea with him he spoke of Rousseau with a kind of religious respect, " Voltaire sought to correct the vices " and the follies of mankind by laughing at " them, and sometimes by treating them " with severity; Rousseau conducts the rea- " der to reason and truth, by the attraction " of sentiment, and the force of conviction. " His *social compact* will one day avenge all " the persecutions he experienced."

He asked me one day, whether I loved music? I answered, that it formed one of my chief delights whenever I was so fortunate as to hear it well executed. "I am very glad of it," said he, " I shall put you to a proof which will " be very interesting for me; for I shall take " you to hear a kind of music of which it is " impossible you can have formed any idea, " and it will afford me great pleasure to know " the impression it makes upon you."

Next morning at nine o'clock, Smith came to my lodgings. At ten he conducted me to a spacious concert-room, plainly but neatly decorated, in which I found a numerous audience. I saw, however, neither orchestra, musicians, nor instruments. A large space was left void in the middle of the room, and

fur-

furrounded with benches which were occupied by gentlemen only. Ladies and gentlemen were difperfed over the room upon other feats. Adam Smith informed me, that the gentlemen who fat in the middle were the judges of the mufical competition which was about to take place; they were almoft all, he obferved, inhabitants of the ifles or highlands of Scotland and might therefore be regarded as the natural judges of the conteft. They were to decree a prize to him who fhould beft execute a favourite piece of Highland Mufic. The fame air was therefore to be played by all the competitors.

In about half an hour, a folding door opened at the bottom of the room, and to my great furprife, I faw a Highlander advance, playing upon the bagpipe. He was dreffed in the ancient Roman habit of his country. He walked up and down the empty fpace with rapid fteps and a martial air, blowing his noify inftrument, the difcordant founds of which were fufficient to rend the ear. The tune was a kind of fonata, divided into three parts. Smith requefted me to pay my whole attention to the mufic, and to explain to him afterwards the impreffion it made upon me.

But

But I confefs that at firft I could not diftinguifh either air or defign in the mufic. I was only ftruck with the piper marching continually backward and forward with great rapidity, and ftill prefenting the fame warlike countenance. He made incredible-efforts with his body and his fingers to bring into play the different reeds of his inftrument, which emitted founds that were to me almoft infupportable.

He received however great applaufe. A fecond mufician fucceeded, who was alfo left alone in the intermediate area, which he traverfed with the fame rapidity as the former. His countenance was no lefs dignified and martial than that of his predeceffor. He appeared to excel the firft competitor; and clapping of hands and cries of *bravo* refounded on every fide. During the third part of the air I obferved that tears flowed from the eyes of a number of the audience.

Having liftened with much attention to eight pipers in fucceffion, I at laft began to difcover that the firft part of the air was a warlike march: the fecond feemed to defcribe a fanguinary action; the mufician endeavouring by a rapid fucceffion of loud and difcordant

dant founds to reprefent the clafhing of arms, the fhrieks of the wounded, and all the horrors of a field of battle. In this part, the performer appeared convulfed; his pantomimical geftures refembled thofe of a man engaged in combat. His arms, his hands, his head, his legs, were all in motion. He called forth all the various founds of his inftrument at the fame moment, and this fingular diforder made a great impreffion upon the company.

With a rapid tranfition the piper paffed to the third part, which was in a kind of andante. His convulfive motions fuddenly ceafed. His countenance affumed an air of deep forrow. The founds of his inftrument were plaintive, languid and melancholy. They were lamentations for the flain—the wailings of their friends who carried them from the field of battle. This was the part which drew tears from the eyes of the beautiful Scotch ladies.

The whole of this entertainment was fo extraordinary, and the impreffion which the founds of this wild inftrument feemed to make upon the greater part of the audience was fo very different from that which they made upon me, that I could not avoid conceiving that the lively emotions exhibited by the perfons sons around me were not occasioned by the musical effect of the air itself, but by an association of ideas which connected the discordant sounds of the bagpipe with some historical facts thus brought forcibly to the recollection of the audience *. There are scarcely any traces of a written language among the Highlanders, either in manuscripts or upon their monuments; it may therefore be presumed that they have had recourse to songs to transmit to their posterity the history of the events in which they were deeply interested. Accustomed to hear these airs from their infancy, and taught by their parents to connect them with transactions which are to them of the greatest importance: they never hear them without being strongly affected. It is not therefore astonishing that they are so passion-

* Johnson makes the following observation on an air which he heard at the seat of Sir Alexander M'Donald in the isle of Sky: "As we sat at Sir Alexander's table, we
" were entertained, according to the ancient usage of the
" North, with the melody of the bagpipe. Every thing in
" those countries has its history As the bagpiper was
" playing, an elderly gentleman informed us, that in some
" remote time, the M'Donalds of Glengary having been
" injured, or offended by the inhabitants of Culloden, and
" resolving to have justice or vengeance, came to Cullo-
" den on a Sunday, where finding their enemies at wor-
" ship, they shut them up in the church, which they set on
" fire; and this, said he, is the tune which the piper
" played while they were burning."

ately

ately fond of this kind of mufic. They have however another kind which is better adapted to the voice, and conftructed more according to the rules of art, which they ufe in their dances, and their amorous and convivial fongs: But they regard this mufic as inferior to the former.

The fame air was played by each competitor, of whom there was a confiderable number. There appeared to be no preference given but to talents, and the moft difinterefted applaufe was beftowed on thofe who excelled in their art. I confefs I did not admire any of them. To me they were all equally difagreeable. The mufic and the inftrument conftantly reminded me of a bear's dance.

The competition was followed by a lively and animated dance, formed by a part of the pipers while the others played fuitable airs, which poffeffed expreffion and character; but the union of fo many bagpipes produced a moft hideous noife.

The competitors afterwards formed themfelves into a line two deep, and marched in that order to the caftle of Edinburgh, which is built upon a volcanic rock. There they played

played an air, which was a kind of ballad, in honour of the unfortunate Mary Queen of Scots, for whom the Highlanders ftill preferve a warm attachment and religious refpect. They fpeak of her with a tender affection: They regard her as the innocent victim of the cruel and implacable jealoufy of Elizabeth. Mary was their Queen. They knew that fhe was beautiful, mild, affable and generous; that fhe loved the arts; that fhe long languifhed in a painful captivity; and that fhe died with refignation and courage. Lefs would be fufficient to intereft honeft peaceable men, whom ftate policy, and the crimes which it engenders, have not yet corrupted, and who abhor the fhedding of blood in any way but for legitimate defence.

I do not know the antiquity of competitions of this kind. During my ftay in Mull, I was informed that there had been beyond all time of memory a college or fociety of bagpipers in that ifland. This fchool was not entirely extinguifhed in confequence of the death of the famous Rankin, who had the direction of it for about thirty years. M'Rimmon kept a fimilar fchool in the ifle of Sky, and each of the principal families of the

the Hebrides always kept a piper, whofe office was hereditary.

While I remained at Edinburgh I made feveral excurfions for the purpofe of examining the natural hiftory of the environs of that city, and I formed a large collection of volcanic fubftances, and other interefting mineralogical fpecimens. Each article was carefully ticketted, and Doctor Swediaur kindly took upon himfelf the charge of fending them to France with the other collections I had made in the Hebrides.

This rich collection, the fruit of fo much pain and fo much pleafure, was loft, as well as the veffel in which it was embarked, on the coaft of Dunkirk. The crew with difficulty faved themfelves in a boat, and I was deprived in a moment of a treafure to which I attached the greater value becaufe it contained a variety of new objects which would have been highly interefting to naturalifts.

Fortunately, whenever I had leifure, I wrote exact defcriptions of the fpecimens I collected, which have enabled me to give a correct account of the lithology of Glafgow, Perth, Staffa, the ifle of Mull, and other places. My various engagements at Edinburgh, however,

ever, did not leave me time to take descriptions of the whole of the specimens I collected there. This is the only omission of the kind I have to charge myself with; but unfortunately it prevents me from giving a complete account of the various and remarkable productions with which the hills that are grouped around that city abound, and which have almost all been a prey to the action of subterraneous fire.

I should have been the more desirous of giving a detailed account of these specimens, which left no doubt as to the existence of ancient volcanos, since I found the greater part of the learned men of this city obstinately prejudiced against this opinion.

The castle, which commands the town, is built upon a hill formed of compact lava in the form of basaltes. The black colour of this lava, and the gothic aspect of the castle which surmounts this volcanic precipice, forms a striking and very pleasing contrast with the elegant white houses, built with great taste in that part of the city which is called the New Town.

Not far from this there is another eminence called the Calton Hill, formed of

greyish

greyish lava, near the top of which there stands a monument erected to the memory of a philosopher and an historian—It contains the ashes of David Hume.

Behind the town there is an elevated chain in a part of which the hills seem piled up one against the other, and are composed of basaltic lava. This substance, which, at one time, must have been liquefied, exhibits prismatic septa occasioned by the cooling of the lava. There is here, however, none of that astonishing regularity displayed in the prismatic columns of the cave of Fingal, or the Giants Causeway of Antrim. The rapid mode in which this lava probably cooled, may have prevented this beautiful effect from taking place, or perhaps that regularity is produced by causes of which we still are ignorant.

One of the hills of this ridge, has a hollow in its summit, and in the whole of its form somewhat resembles a chair or gigantic seat. This spot, in which there is nothing remarkable but its elevation and its steepness, is known in the Old Chronicles under the latin name of *Arthuri Sedes*, and

and in English by that of *Arthur's Seat*. It is possible, however, that this name may have its origin in some other cause than the figure of the top of the hill, the tradition of which is lost.

Sibbald, in his *Scotia Illustrata*, printed in 1684, gives an account of a barometrical observation made by the mathematician, George Sinclair, on the summit and at the bottom of a mountain which he calls *Sedes Arthuri*. There is no doubt but it is the same as that of which I have been speaking *.

I examined the large blocks of basaltes which are detached from this mountain and lie scattered about at its base, in which I observed spots of zeolite even in the centre of the lava. I collected some very fine specimens. This zeolite which is white, and

---

* Ex observatione Georgii Sinclari mathematici nostratis, in vertice illius montis, cui nomen vulgo ARTHURI SEDES, ob id imprimis celebris, quod civitati Edinburgi, ob vicinitatem imminet, mercurialis cylindri altitudo reperta est 28, digitorum cum quadrante; apud radices autem montis 29. Sibbald, Scotia Illustrata, par I. lib. i. folio 10.

in fome parts clouded with a blueifh tinge, is neither radiated nor cryftallized in a regular manner. It is rather of the fcaly texture of white marble. It is hard and fufceptible of the moft brilliant polifh. This is not furprifing, when it is confidered that it contains a fmall mixture of quartzofe earth. This gives it fomething of a calcedonious appearance; but it is fufible with the blowpipe, bubbles in fmelting, and has all the properties of zeolite.

Behind thefe volcanized mountains there are beds of quartzofe free-ftone, which has experienced in a very confiderable degree the action of fire, and thereby acquired a reddifh colour. Indeed; the operation of fubterraneous fire is manifeft every where around Edinburgh, where it exhibits the fame characteriftic traces as in the environs of Perth, Glafgow, and Dunbarton, and in the ifland of Staffa.

1 regret that I am obliged to confine myfelf to this general defcription: If my valuable collection had not been loft, I fhould have defcribed a feries of volcanic productions which would have removed every doubt on this fubject, and demonftrated

strated that the vicinity of Edinburgh has been the prey of ancient volcanos, since it still exhibits lavas similar to those of Etna and Vesuvius.

CHAPTER XV.

Departure from Edinburgh.—Itinerary to Manchester.—Natural History

AFTER taking leave of Doctors Black, Cullen, Smith, and the other refpectable characters who had treated me with fo much kindnefs in Edinburgh, I made preparations for my return to London; I determined to take the Carlifle road, which would give me an opportunity of feeing Manchefter, Derby, Buxton, Caftleton, Birmingham, &c.

When I left London with my fellow-travellers our party confifted of four perfons, on returning from Edinburgh it was reduced to two.

I forgot to mention that M. de Mecies, after vifiting the cave of Fingal, which was the principal object of his journey, left us at Mr. M'Lean's, in the ifle of Mull, and fet out for London, where bufinefs required his prefence.

Our other interefting and agreeable fellow-traveller William Thornton, intending

to

to pafs fome months with his friends in America, determined to remain in Edinburgh, where he had a numerous acquaintance, until he fhould find a veffel to carry him to his native country. We feparated from him with much pain, for his excellent moral qualities, and his love for the fciences, rendered him truly amiable and worthy of all our attachment.

All our bufinefs being at laft arranged, Count Andreani and I left Edinburgh on the 3d of October, taking the Carlifle road.

About a mile and a half from Edinburgh, the lavas and other volcanic fubftances which furround that city, difappear: they are fucceeded by quartzofe free-ftone, which in feveral places cover rich mines of coal. This fandy zone, which is pretty extenfive, difappears in its turn, and the face of the country again exhibits volcanic fubftances from Laffwade to Selkirk, in paffing through Middleton, Bankhoufe, Stagehall, Crofslee, &c.

The afpect of this part of the country is wild and fterile. The black, blueifh, and reddifh brown lavas which we obferved on the road, were almoft all difpofed in tables or plates like flate; but they had all experienced

rienced the action of fire, some were of the nature of basaltes; but others, which were less hard, exfoliated and decomposed in the air.

We proceeded on to Arnskirk, Hawick, Allanmouth, Binks, Redpath, and Langholm. The mile-stone at this last place is marked 69 from Edinburgh. Volcanic appearances prevail from Arnskirk to Langholm. The lavas at Hawick form steep hills, and are disposed in horizontal beds, or rather lamellæ, which resemble slate; their colour, however, is more pale. There is little doubt but that all the hills and mountains in this quarter have experienced the action of fire.

Kirk-Andrews, Longtown, Westlington, Carlisle.—Sand and quartzose free-stone of an ochreous red colour—fine cultivation in the neighbourhood of Carlisle—large and excellent ploughs—a number of kilns for making lime, which is used for manure. Lime is not only used for the meadows, but also for the arable land; small heaps are formed which are allowed to slack in the air, and are afterwards spread over the fields.

A ſtage before we arrived at Carliſle, we had a view of Solway Frith, which ſeparates England from Scotland on the Weſt.

Haraby, Carleton, Lowheſketh, Higheſketh. The ſame materials as above, that is to ſay, ſand, red quartzoſe, free-ſtone, and calcareous ſtones.

Perith. At a mile from this town, on the declivity of a mountain, there are large rounded blocks of baſaltic lava, intermixed with maſſes of granite, which are alſo rounded.

Eumont Bridge, Cliſton, Thrimby. Blocks of reddiſh granite of a conſiderable ſize, with ſome rounded baſaltes, both placed upon beds of calcareous ſtone.

Shap, Hauſefoot. Here the hills of tabulated and foliated lava re-appear. Some of them reſemble thoſe of Mount-Mezen, in Velai, which I have deſcribed in my *Mineralogie des Volcans.*

Kendal, Syzergh. The ſame volcanic appearances.

Haverſham, Milthorpe, Holme, Burton, Dure-Bridge, Carnford, Bolton, Slyne, Lancaſter. This road is almoſt entirely through a calcareous country; rounded baſaltes are, however,

however, fometimes found fcattered in the fields. The country is in general rich in pafture. The meadows are manured with a mixture of lime, dung, and common earth, which forms an excellent compoft.

From Lancafter we proceeded to Manchefter.

CHAPTER XVI.

Manchester.—Doctor Henry and his Cabinet.—Cotton Manufactures.—Meſſieurs Thomas and Benjamin Potter.—Charles Taylor.

IT was late when we arrived at Mancheſter. As I had letters to Doctors White and Percival, I wrote to them next morning, requeſting to know at what hour it would be convenient for them to ſee me, but it happened that they were both obliged to viſit patients at the diſtance of ſome miles from the town. Doctor Percival ſent a young German of his acquaintance to ſtate the regret he felt in conſequence of not being able to ſee us; and Doctor White engaged his friend, Doctor Henry, to wait upon us in his ſtead. Theſe two gentlemen had the complaiſance to offer every ſervice in their power, and to ſhew us whatever was remarkable in the town. They paid us the moſt polite attention, and never left us during the ſtay we made in Mancheſter.

Mancheſter is a large town; it contains between thirty-ſix and forty thouſand inhabitants;

tants; but if the manufacturers who live in its environs were added to this number, the population would be greatly increased, and might be ranked with that of most cities of the second order.

The old cathedral is large and well built. We saw also some other structures of this kind which were not uninteresting: the cotton-mills, however, which have enriched this town, were objects still more worthy of engaging our attention.

But notwithstanding the desire of our kind conductors to oblige us we found it impossible to see any thing of the kind. Every attempt was vain. The vigilance of the manufacturers was redoubled in consequence of having persuaded themselves that a French colonel, who was there some time before us, wanted to procure plans of these machines in order to carry them to France. Since that period no strangers, not even the most respectable citizens of the town were permitted to enter the works *.

The

---

* At this time the machine for carding cotton had already been carried to France and was used there. Not long after the mills were introduced by an intelligent English-

The largeſt of theſe cotton-mills are moved by water: they ſpin the cotton to ſo much perfection, and with ſo much economy, that thoſe who firſt erected them have made great fortunes. Arkwright, who invented them, was merely a barber, in the town of Manchester. The difficulties he muſt have had to ſurmount in that ſituation, doubtleſs, add to his merit. He had the good ſenſe to turn his diſcovery to profit. He joined in company with manufacturers whom he enriched, and at the ſame time made a great fortune himſelf.

Though I had not an opportunity of ſeeing the cotton-mills, I was, however, very complaiſantly ſhewn large warehouſes full of manufactured goods. The fineſt pieces were unfolded in order that I might ſee the patterns and the colours. We entered into converſation on the chymical proceſſes uſed in

Engliſhman, who diſputed the merit of the invention with Arkwright. Theſe ingenious machines are now erected in ſeveral departments where they are conſtantly employed. This manufacture will doubtleſs be carried on with ſpirit, until caprice and faſhion return to the uſe of ſilk, that beautiful and ſumptuous production of France, which employed ſuch a number of hands and yielded revenues ſo immenſe.

dying

dying the colours with very intelligent men, particularly with Meffrs. Thomas and Benjamin Potter, and Mr. Taylor, who treated us in the moſt affable manner. It is with pleaſure I here expreſs the gratitude I feel for their kindneſs.

We were doubtleſs indebted to Doctor Henry for all the politeneſs that was ſhewn to us in Mancheſter. I wiſh that I may one day have an opportunity of making a return to his kindneſs in France. He tranſlated the works of Lavoiſier into Engliſh, and ſtudies chymiſtry much more than natural hiſtory. At his houſe, however, I ſaw ſome ſtones and minerals; but that which gave me the greateſt pleaſure in his collection was a fine foſſile Os femoris, of the unknown animal whoſe bones are found on the banks of the Ohio, and which is perhaps only a loſt ſpecies of the elephant. This Os femoris, which was in the moſt perfect preſervation, weighed forty pounds.

CHAPTER XVII.

Departure from Manchester.—Buxton; its Mineral Waters; fine Baths, constructed on a Plan by Carr, at the Expence of the Duke of Devonshire, the Proprietor of the Waters.—Doctor Pearson.— Manufacture of Vases and other Articles in Fluor Spar of different Colours.—Cave of Poole's Hole.— Toad-stone, composed of a Basis of Trapp, interspersed with Particles of calcareous Spar, and cracked into prismatic Sections like those of basaltes, though not produced by Fire as the latter has been.

WE were received in a very polite manner, as I have already observed, by Doctor Henry, and those to whom he was good enough to introduce us. But we did not experience an equally kind treatment from the master of the *Bull's Head* inn, where we had put up. For two sorry dinners he charged us no less than seventeen shillings a-piece, to which we had to add three shillings to his servants; and this was exclusive of the bill for our domestics. The best thing that poor strangers can do in such a case is to pay the money. Travellers are equally liable to this sort of exaction in Italy, Germany,

Germany, and France, as in England; but in neither is it general or derived from national character. It muſt be imputed to a few individuals only, who have loſt all feelings of delicacy and juſtice, but who make a very wrong calculation with reſpect to their real intereſts, as they ſoon deſtroy both their own reputation and that of the houſes they keep. It is a very difficult matter to deviſe good regulations of police upon this ſubject. It is a truth well known to ſuch as are in the habit of travelling, that the charges are always higheſt at thoſe inns where the entertainment is the worſt. It is to be hoped that ſome remedy will be found for this abuſe; but in the mean time it will be neceſſary for travellers to keep a ſeparate purſe for thoſe plundering inn-keepers, as is done in England for thoſe *gentlemen* who rob on the highways, to whom thoſe who venture to travel at late hours give without fear or danger the ſum which is ſet apart for them. I muſt ſay for my part, however, that I paſſed through England and Scotland twice, and by different roads, without meeting any of theſe *gentlemen*; and that I experienced no extortion but at two places, *Dun's Hotel* in Edinburgh,

burgh, and the *Bull's Head* in Manchester.

From Manchester to Buxton is twenty-four miles. The road through Derbyshire is neither agreeable nor commodious. It sometimes crosses over craggy mountains, and at others runs along narrow, wet and dirty valleys, and though the turnpikes are numerous and dear, the roads are notwithstanding in a bad condition. They are in general, however, well supplied with post-horses. We left Manchester at seven in the morning, and did not reach Buxton till two in the afternoon.

Buxton is remarkable for its mineral waters, for the benefit of which a considerable afflux of company repair thither in the fine season. Buxton, however, is situated in the midst of the most dismal and cheerless country that I have ever seen. Its waters may be excellent, but most certainly its atmosphere is impregnated with sadness and melancholy. The houses, almost entirely of a uniform appearance, but solid construction, resemble hospitals or rather monastic establishments. A superb structure, executed in a grand and beautiful stile of architecture, which appears

at

at the bottom of the place, and is appropriated to the baths, might be taken for the palace of the abbot.

We had letters of recommendation for Doctor Pearson, a London Phyfician, who belongs to the eftablishment of the baths of Buxton, where he generally spends six months of the year. We were fortunate enough to find him there, though it was now pretty late in the feafon. As he was well acquainted with the country, and had publifhed an analyfis of the waters, in which he defcribed the stones and earths that form the foil of Buxton, he kindly and readily offered to conduct us to the moft remarkable mines and caverns, the noted beds of lime-ftone, in his opinion, interfected with feveral currents of lava, and to the different other places mentioned in his book.

Doctor Pearfon was very intimate with Whitehurft, and had adopted his opinion refpecting the beds of toad-ftone, which he regarded as the product of fubterraneous fire*. We fixed a day for going to fee thefe fup-

* *Obfervations and experiments on Buxton Waters, &c. By Doctor Pearfon. London.*

pofed

posed remains of volcanos in a country, where, on the contrary, every thing indicates the agency of water; and he had the goodness, in the mean time, to accompany us to the shops of several artists in stone, who cut, turn, and polish the fine Derbyshire fluor or phosphoric spars * of different colours, gypseous alabasters, and some marbles.

WORKERS IN FLUOR OR PHOSPHORIC SPAR.

Several artists in this line have settled at Buxton on account of the numerous and in general opulent visitants who resort thither for the waters, and whose fancy or taste inclines them to purchase their productions. The fluor spars are turned into small hollow or solid vases, columns, eggs, pears, and watches, and cut into pyramids, pedestals, &c. As the colours are beautiful and variegated, and the stone is susceptible of a fine shining polish, it was formerly sold at a very high rate; but since it has been found in so great abundance, the increase of artificers, and the consequent competition among each other,

* The *Fluas calcareus* of the new nomenclature of chymistry, page 172.

have

have contributed to diminish very much the price of these articles of ornament. There are very few among the stone-cutters of Buxton who shew any taste for the beautiful forms. They have signs above their shop-doors with their names and the addition of *petrifaction-works.*

The most intelligent of them, in my opinion, was one Noel, who was in easy circumstances, and had succeeded well in this branch of trade. He was bringing up to the same art a daughter and a son, who were already almost as well skilled in it as himself, though the boy was only eight, and the girl nine years of age. It was at his shop that the best turned vases were to be seen.

Samuel Cooper had the best stocked shop; but his pieces were dearer than those of the others.

John Evans and Mottershed, are two other artificers who have pretty good assortments.

It is necessary to guard against a number of little contrivances which they make use of to repair the accidents which sometimes happen to their productions, and consequently to deceive the purchasers.

They

They introduce, for inftance, into the accidental cavities or fractures, which they are dextrous enough at repairing, quantities of lead in its native ftate, that is, as it comes from the mine. They then polifh it; and are not wanting in affurances to the purchafer that it is natural to the fpar, and enhances its value.

I remarked alfo, that to give a finer luftre to their productions, they had always fome water at hand to plunge them into, on the pretence that it was only to wafh off the duft. But it was eafily feen that the water had a fingular effect in enlivening the colours, the polifh, and the femi-tranfparency of the ftone.

The fluor fpar, which is fafhioned at Buxton, is procured from the lead mines of Caftleton, about ten miles from the former. The only ftones of value found in the environs of Buxton, are a very fine gypfeous, white, femi-tranfparent alabafter, which is made into vafes and pedeftals, a black marble emitting a bituminous fmell on being rubbed, and a yellowifh calcareous fpar, both of which are applied to the fame purpofe.

THE

THE BATH-HOUSE.

This superb edifice has more the appearance of a palace than that of a place for bathing. It is a vaſt fabric, in the ſhape of a rotunda, ornamented all round on the outſide with large pilaſters which ſupport a rich cornice crowned with a balluſtrade.

This building, in addition to the ſpace occupied by the baths, contains apartments for more than two hundred gentlemen, excluſively of the chambers for their domeſtics, the perſons employed about the baths and wells, and the different maſters of taverns and ordinaries neceſſary to provide for ſo numerous an aſſemblage, and who are the principal renters of the whole ſtructure. It contains alſo coffee-rooms, gaming-rooms, and ball-rooms.

The whole of this vaſt fabric was erected at the expence of the duke of Devonſhire, upon the plans and under the ſuperintendance of the architect Carr. It is executed in an excellent ſtile of architecture, uniting to a character of grandeur an air of taſte, which does honour to the talents of that able artiſt, whom

I had

I had the pleasure of seeing, and who was kind enough to conduct me through every part of it.

The baths are difposed with the fame judgment as the other parts of the work. There are common and private ones for the women; those for the men are in a feparate quarter and poffefs the fame conveniencies. There are feveral alfo appropriated to the ufe of the poor.

The mineral waters for drinking run into a large ciftern of white marble, over which is erected a neat little temple finely executed in an antique ftile.

The waters of Buxton are rather moderately warm than hot; as they do not raife the mercury in Farhenheits thermometer above eighty-two degrees. Doctor Pearfon, who has analized them, fays, " that the air which is extricated " from it in great abundance, does not contain " any fixed air, but atmofpheric mephits, or " the *azotic gas* of the new nomenclature *."
This is a very remarkable fact.

The

---

* The term azot, is derived from the Greek, and fignifies the privation of life; but, as other gas produce the fame effect, the word is improper. I do not mean to attack

The village of Buxton is not very confiderable, and the greater part of the houfes are the property of the duke of Devonſhire. They are generally rented by tavern-keepers, and yield him a great revenue. The one neareſt the baths lets for twelve hundred pounds ſterling; and, I was affured, that the baths alone produce a yearly rent of at leaſt thirty-fix thouſand French livres.

To draw a greater number to the houfes belonging to himſelf, the duke of Devonſhire adopted a plan which has met with complete fuccefs. Thofe who are lodged in any of them are charged only ten-pence Englifh a-day, for the waters, whilſt fuch as have apartments elfewhere pay a fhilling a-day.

LITHOLOGY OF THE ENVIRONS OF BUXTON.

Buxton is fituated in the midſt of a number of ſmall hills, which are quite clofe to

---

tack the principles of pnumatic chymiſtry, but its language only. If this malady, which is as dreadful to the language of Racine, Fenelon, Bouffon, Voltaire, &c. as the leprofy is to the beauty of a fine woman, gains ground in the other fciences, we fhall foon realize the fable of the tower of Babel. A confufion of language will introduce a confufion of ideas; and we fhall thus be replunged in the gloom of barbarifm.

each other, and the higheſt of which does not exceed ſix hundred and fifty feet. The fine river Wye takes its riſe at a little diſtance from the elegant ſtructure of the new baths; and ſoon after plunges into a deep chaſm, and winds along between two approaching cliffs.

The mountains on the road from Buxton to Man‑heſter are compoſed of banks of free-ſtone, in ſome parts hard and in others ſoft and friable, and ſometimes foliated. The hard kind, beſides the name of free-ſtone, is here called *greet*, *grit*, and ſometimes *mill-ſtone-greet*; the foliated kind is termed *ſlate*. Theſe free-ſtones are diſpoſed ſometimes in large horizontal banks, and at other times in foliated ſtrata; they are in general white or reddiſh.

Near theſe, and almoſt oppoſite to them, are hills entirely formed of lime-ſtone in horizontal beds in ſome places, and in a continuous uninterrupted maſs in others. Theſe maſſes are ſometimes divided by perpendicular or diagonal fiſſures.

This lime-ſtone is hard, almoſt of a ſparry texture, and yields on being burnt a lime of a very fine quality. It is uſed,

as

as well as free-ftone, for making door-cafes, chimney-pieces, pedeftals, and other works. Its colour is in fome quarries whitifh or greyifh, and in others black. The latter is employed for the fame purpofes as marble; and it fcarcely contains any marine body. It exhales a very difagreeable fmell on being rubbed; it may be regarded as a kind of pierrepore.

The grey, on the contrary, contains madrepores, entrochi, and other marine petrifactions. There are alfo found in it fome pieces of filex which are full of entrochitæ. The grey calcareous ftratum does not poffefs the fame degree of hardnefs throughout. The foft part emits a difagreeable fmell on being rubbed, not fo ftrong, indeed, as that of the black kind, but ftill very fenfible. The harder pieces of the grey fort are ufed for feveral domeftic purpofes. I fhall refume the confideration of thefe calcareous beds, which are remarkable for the circumftance of being interrupted with alternate beds of toad-ftone.

There is alfo found in that part of Derbyfhire called the *Peak*, in which is fituated Buxton, Matlock, Wirkefworth, Middleton,

Maffon

Maffon Crumford, Winfter, Caftleton, Eyam, &c. black argillaceous fchiftus, more or lefs hard, and fometimes refembling flate, or as it is here called *fhale* or *fhiver*, black and grey martial argil, more or lefs hard, which is not applied to any ufe, and which bears the name of *iron-ftone*, and red and grey marl, befides a brownifh kind of marl of a very fine grain, and loaded with calcareous particles, which is ufed like tripoli for polifhing tin, copper, cryftal, &c. this kind is called *rotten-ftone*. In this tract are alfo feveral mines of coal, which are worked in abundance. They are not however very deep in general; their roof is a black argillaceous fchiftus, marked with numerous prints of ferns, the greater part of which feem to be foreign. Here are likewife found pyrites, black marble, grey marble, foft lime-ftone, free-ftone, compact, gypfum, ftriated gypfum, fluor fpar of the appearance of amethyft, yellow, red, grey, or white; and a ponderous fine grained white earth which may be cut as eafily as chalk, is faid to abound in gypfeous earth, and is indifferently termed *caulk, calk, cawk, kewel,* and *keble*. This matter is one of the moft common matrices of the mines of Derbyfhire, and is frequently

quently feen adhering to fluor fpar*. To the above enumeration may be added double pointed rock cryftals, ponderous fpar, and opake fluor fpar, in detached cubical cryftals, which three fubftances are found on Diamond Hill, about three miles from Buxton ; calcareous tolfa, with feveral plants incrufted in it, manganefs in kidney-fhaped lumps, lead, copper, calamine, and blende ; the wells of Matlock old bath, Matlock new bath, and Buxton ; the acidulated mineral waters of Quarn, or Quarnden, an intermitting fpring at Tidefwell, and a number of natural grottos or caverns, feveral of which penetrate to a great extent, fuch as thofe of Caftleton, Poole's-hole, Elden-hole, Hofen's-hole, Burmforth-hole, and Lathkill-arfe. It is very remarkable that pretty copious ftreams of water iffue from almoft all of thefe caverns.

Such is a brief fketch of the principal objects obferved in the Peak of Derbyfhire ; and this aftonifhing variety of fubftances within

* It is thought that the *caulk* makes the regulus of antimony more ductile, and gives it a compact texture. It is ufed at Birmingham in the manufactury of yellow copper. Some perfons imagine that it is for the purpofe of molds, but of this there is no certainty, the greater part of the proceffes being concealed in the Englifh manufactories.

so small a compass, must certainly astonish the most experienced geologists. We accordingly find Mr. Ferber, so well known for his "*Letters on the Mineralogy of Italy,*" in the preface to a pamphlet which he has published on that of Derbyshire, acknowle'g ng that, without the aid of Mr. Whitehurst and Mr. Burdett, who has published a fine map of Derbyshire, he should have been completely bewildered amidst the production of so singular a country.

"I sincerely acknowledge," says he, "that
"without the assistance of these two persons,
"I should have frequently found it very diffi-
"cult to explain a great number of phæno-
"mena which were quite new to me. I
"had till then seen only homogeneous moun-
"tains; and none of the stratified mountains
"which I had examined, and of the interior
"structure of which I had perfect knowledge
"by visiting the mines, furnished any in-
"stance to be compared with what I saw in
"Derbyshire. The great diversity of the
"strata and their frequently fantastic dispo-
"sition which I had never seen any where
"else, very often embarrassed me; and I am
"persuaded

" perſuaded that the ableſt mineralogiſts will
" experience the ſame difficulty *."

THE CAVE OF POOL'S-HOLE.

Mr. Ferber, in his " *Eſſay on the Orycto-*
" *graphy of Derbyſhire,*" does no more than
ſlightly mention the cave of Pool's-hole.
" This cave," ſays he, " which is at a little
" diſtance from Buxton, abounds in ſtalactite.
" It is ſaid to be half an Engliſh league in
" length, and a very noiſy ſtream runs
" through it."

The following is a more minute deſcription:—Pool's-hole is about a mile from Buxton; and its entrance is at the foot of a large hill conſiſting of lime-ſtone, bare on all ſides, and preſenting to the view a number of kilns, where the ſtone, which is of an excellent quality, is burnt into lime. This limeſtone contains a number of entrochi and other marine bodies, converted for the moſt part into calcareous ſpar.

Doctor Pearſon was ſo obliging as to accompany us to the cave. Scarcely had we

* *Eſſai ſur l'Oryctographie du Derbyſhire, province d'Angleterre, par M. Ferber, traduction de l'Allemand.*

arrived at the mouth of it, which is narrow and of an oblong fhape, when we were joined by feveral women who made brifkly up to us; fome of them, to fell us pieces of bad ftalactite and fhining calcareous fpar; and others to furnifh us with lights, and to offer their fervices in the capacity of guides. We accepted their offers, and entered the cave. Here, as in almoft all natural caves, are galleries fometimes narrow, and at others broad, now winding and then running in a ftraight line, and at intervals expanding into fpacious and lofty chambers. We were defired by our guides to ftop when we came oppofite to a very large ftalagmite, which is only an irregular and confufed accumulation of calcareous fpar depofited by the droppings.

This is called by the natives *Poole's chair.* They have heard it termed fo by their fathers, thofe who fucceed them will give it the fame appellation; and though this fparry mafs has no more refemblance to a chair than it has to a horfe, the power of imagination and habit, will concur in maintaining this abfurdity, and thofe good folks will always have the fatisfaction of thinking that they fee what they do not fee. Alas! this is the cafe

cafe with refpect to many other things in this world.

On penetrating into a more profound cavity, our conductors were not wanting in telling us that this was *Poole's chamber*; and a little farther we were fhewn *Poole's table**.

The cave is about two thoufand four hundred and fifty Englifh feet in length, including the paffages into it, fome of which are very incommodious. A fmall ftream of water, which becomes more confiderable perhaps in rainy feafons, runs through the whole length of the galleries, and makes the way a little difagreeable. Upon the whole, this cave contains nothing very interefting. We faw in it only a few bad and mutilated ftalactites, and thefe not in any great quantity. From the fhock of an earthquake, or the loofenefs and weight of the incumbent mafs, part of the roof of one of the galleries has fallen in, and the paffage is almoft entirely blocked up by the number and bulk of the ftones which have tumbled down.

---

* Credulity has always amufed herfelf with feeing fomething marvellous in thefe dark fubterraneous caverns. There is ftill fhewn in the cave of Saffenage, near Grenoble, the famous table of the fairy Mellufina.

On coming out of the cave, we were anew surrounded by some women, who offered for sale some coarse pieces of cryftallized calcareous spar, to which they seemed to affix a great value.

We then visited the numerous quarries of lime-ftone dug on all parts of the hill, which contains the cave of Poole's-hole. More than a undred families have been occupied, from father to son, in working the quarries and converting the ftones into lime. The consumption of this article muft be extensive, and the demand for it very great, for limekilns are seen smoking on every side.

I looked in vain for the habitations of so many labourers and their numerous families, without being able to see so much as one cottage, when I at length difcerned that the whole tribe, like so many moles, had formed their residence under ground. This comparison is ftrictly juft; not one individual of them lodged in a houfe, or even the hollow of a rock. Their dwellings were in the midft of heaps of cinders and refufe of lime, which formed so many small mounts, or mole-hills.

Thefe

These materials, which the workmen have hollowed into subterraneous habitations, have been consolidated by rain into a compact cement which is now impenetrable to the water. As the excavation is not very difficult, these families have taken sufficient precaution against cold and wet, by fixing their abode immediately contiguous to the lime-kilns which communicate to them a comfortable degree of warmth.

The greater part of these habitations have three or four rooms, almost all of a round form, for the purpose of greater solidity. They are lighted by the side, when the position is such as to admit it; or merely by the chimney, which is nothing else than a round hole pierced through the middle of the roof to allow the smoke to escape. Apertures are also made by the door of the place to admit a little light. Such is the effect of the whole, that when the workmen descend into their cave, at the hours of repast, nd a stranger sees so many small columns of smoke issuing out of the earth, he imagines himself in the midst of a village in Lapland. I felt much pleasure in visiting the residence of these troglodytes. Their occupation is certainly not attended
with

with much profi as they are unable to procure the fmalleft convenience, and though in the midft of ftones and lime, have hitherto been too poor to erect walls.

STONES KN WN IN DERBYSHIRE BY THE NAME OF TOAD-STONE.

As I had now reached the principal fource of thefe ftones, fo much talked of by the Englifh Naturalifts, and which furnifhed the bafis of Mr. Whitehurft's theory, I refolved to examine them with the moft fcrupulous attention. I had the advantage of being accompanied by a mineralogift of the fchool of Mr. Whitehurft, who was well acquainted with the place, and who, like him, was convinced that the different fpecies of toad-ftone were real lavas. I was under a promife, befides, of giving an account of my refearches to Mr. Whitehurft himfelf. Being provided with his book, and Mr. Ferber's effay on the oryctography of Derbyfhire, the only remaining preparation requifite was the inftructing myfelf in the vocabulary of the miners. The names which they have at all times given this ftone, vary according to its colour, its hardnefs,

nefs, he extraneous bodies found in it, and the difpofition of its ftrata. Thefe names are not fcientific, it is true; but the miners are accuftomed to them, and perfectly underftand them, being derived from their native language; and it is not to be fuppofed that they will ever be induced to change them.

This ftone derives its name from its refemblance to the colour of a *toad*, having a very dark brown and fometimes black, bafis entirely fprinkled over with fmall particles of white calcareous fpar. Thefe white fpecks are in general, pretty uniform, and fometimes protuberant. A ftone in every refpect fimilar is found in the bed of the torrent of Drac, near Grenoble, by which it is hurried along from the high Alps of Champfaur. It is from this fpotted appearance that it has received the name of *Variolite du Drac*. But this term already affixed to a ftone of a different fort, ought to be rejected, in order to prevent miftakes.

The term toad-ftone is very common at Buxton, Matlock and Winfter, becaufe ftones of this kind are more frequent there than in the other lead or copper mines of Derbyfhire.

At

At Tidefwell, the fame ftone, but with few or no globules of calcareous fpar, and difpofed in thick banks, which alternate with beds of lime-ftone, bears the name of *channe*.

At Afhover, in the mine of Gregori, being of a blacker kind and not fo hard, it is called *black clay*.

At Caftletown, the miners have given to a greenifh variety of this ftone, which falls into earth on expofure to the air, the fingular name of *cat-dirt*.

Mr. Ferber, in his effay on the oryctography of Derbyfhire, pages 163 and 168, mentions only the two denominations of *toad-ftone* and *channel*; but he adds, that the fame ftone bears in England the names of *dun-ftone* and *black-ftone*, and in Scotland, that of *whin-ftone*. It is certain that the Derbyfhire miners know very well how to apply the four different names which they give it, according to its different modifications. This is not the cafe with refpect to the Englifh term *black-ftone*, which may be equally applied to other ftones of the fame colour, but of a very different nature, fuch as volcanic bafaltes, touch-ftone, black rock-fchorl, horn-ftone, certain

fine

fine grained black granites, &c. This denomination is, therefore, too general and vague.

The term *whin-stone*, which the Scotch employ, is no lefs objectionable. Under this name they comprehend every black ftone, without diftinction, which is hard and rough to the touch. At Edinburgh, when I afked the naturalifts and workmen of the country to fhew me whin-ftone, fome of them brought me a black hard ftone of the fame nature with what the Swedes call trapp, which is not in the leaft volcanic, fome prefented a compact lava of the nature of bafaltes, and others a variety of black granite, which has fuftained the action of fubterraneous fire without any alteration in its hardnefs, and which makes moft excellent pavements. The cafe was the fame at Glafgow. This term, then, having like the preceding, a variety of acceptations, which tend to produce confufion in the mind, ought to be rejected on the fame account. A fact worthy of remark, and which proves that the colour of ftone has been more attended to than any other characteriftic, is, that in Germany, where the fcience of mineralogy has long flourifhed, feveral black hard ftones, of very different

different natures, are likewife denominated *black-ftones*, fchwartz-ftein *.

Mr. Ferber, though profoundly verfed in mineralogy, neither compares the toad-ftone of Derbyfhire to any other ftone, gives it any diftinctive name, nor takes any notice of the opinion of Mr. Whitehurft, who regards it as a volcanic product. He contents himfelf with ftating, that " this ftone has an argil-
" laceous bafis more or lefs hard ; fome parts
" appearing to be merely an indurated clay,
" whilft others approach the jafper in hard-
" nefs ; that it is interfperfed with fmall par-
" ticles of calcareous fpar, varying in form
" and fize ; fome of which are fo minute
" that to the eye they appear identified with
" the black fubftance of the ftone itfelf, whilft
" others are of the bignefs of a pea, or even a
" bean." He adds, " that on trying the ftone

---

* In France, as in other places, we have in feveral inftances given names to mountains from the colour of their rocks ; fuch as roche *maure* for roche noire (black rock) roque *brune peire neir*, for roche brune (brown rock) pierre noire (black ftone) &c. But on every occafion when I have fhewed to peafants of any degree of intelligence, pieces of compact lava, and blocks or columns of bafaltes, and afked them how they termed thofe ftones, they have uniformly replied, that they were *pierres mortes* (*dead ftones.*)

" with

"with acids, they effervefced with and dif-
"folved the portions of calcareous fpar with-
"out effecting any change in the bafis of the
"ftone; which, after the experiment, was
"ftill hard enough to fcratch glafs, though it
"gave only a few inconfiderable fparks with
"fteel; and finally, that the fubftance of the
"toad-ftone, when divefted of its calcareous
"particles, feemed to him to be refractory to
"the blow-pipe, but that with the addition
"of falt of tartar it was converted into a
"black fcoria, which would feem to indicate a
"filiceous principle, though it does not poffefs
"the hardnefs of filiceous ftones."

To enable thofe naturalifts, who have not vifited the place, to form a correct notion of this ftone, and to accompany me in the following examination, it only remains that I fhould give them a preliminary defcription of the fingular pofition which it occupies in the mountains of the Peak of Derbyfhire. A part of the details I fhall borrow from Mr. Whitehurft and Mr. Ferber, adding to them what additional circumftances have fallen under my own obfervation.

DIFFERENT SUBSTANCES WHICH PRECEDE AND ACCOMPANY THE TOAD-STONE OF THE PEAK OF DERBYSHIRE.

1. Quartzofe greet, gret, or free-ftone; termed mill-ftone by Mr. Whitehurft from the ufe to which it is applied in fome places; it varies in its colour, grain, hardnefs, and the thicknefs of its ftrata. This naturalift, in in page 147 of his " Inquiry into the original ftate and formation of the Earth, fays, " that " the bank is 120 yards in thicknefs, and com-
" pofed of granulated quartz and quartz peb-
" bles. The former retain the fharpnefs of
" fragments newly broken, the latter are
" rounded by attrition as ftones upon a fea
" beach."

2. Black argillaceous fchiftus of the nature of flate, fhale or fhiver. Its thicknefs, according to Mr. Ferber, who meafured it in the mine of Yateftoop, is from a hundred and forty to a hundred and fifty feet*; and according to Mr. Whitehurft, who meafured it in another place, about a hundred and twenty yards †. As it is ufeful, when giving a local defcription, to be acquainted with the nomenclature of the miners, it is proper to ftate that

* Page 160. † Page 148.

they

they give the toad-ftone feveral denominations according to its greater or lefs hardnefs, or as it is more or lefs penetrable. Hence the various terms of *fhale, hard-beds, penny-fhale,* and *black-beds.*

There are found above this fchiftus at feveral places, and, among others, near Winfter, where the high-way is opened through beds of it, which are completely vifible, large fragments of black lime-ftone, which on being rubbed with iron, emits a ftrong fmell of burnt corn.

3. The firft bed of lime-ftone, which, in the neighbourhood of Dafhford, is black, very hard and ufed as marble. It has an offenfive fmell on being rubbed, is in fome parts without any marine bodies, and in others abounds in *anonymæ bivalves*; it fometimes contains round knobs of filex, and is interfected at intervals with thin layers of a kind of flate. The thicknefs of this bank varies from thirty-five to fifty feet.

4. Firft bed of toad-ftone. The thicknefs of this bed varies greatly: in fome places it is fourteen, and in others fixteen feet, and at Tidefwell it has been dug to the depth of a hundred and fixty feet without reaching its bottom; though, in the fame mine, at the diftance

diſtance of a hundred toiſes only from this ſpot, it is no more than forty feet; and three hundred toiſes farther, only three feet. This would ſeem to ſhew that the matter which compoſes the toad-ſtone has accumulated there rather in one vaſt depoſit than in regular beds.

But let us hear Mr. Whitehurſt, whoſe opinion upon this ſtone is very explicit: " Toad-ſtone is a blackiſh ſubſtance, very " hard; contains bladder-holes like the *ſcoria* " of metals, or Iceland lava, and has the ſame " chymical property of reſiſting acids. Some " of its bladder-holes are filled with [cal- " careous] ſpar, others only in part, and others " again are quite empty. This *ſtratum* is not " laminated, but conſiſts of one entire ſolid " maſs, and breaks alike in all directions. It " does not produce any minerals or figured " ſtones repreſenting any part of the animal " or vegetable creation.—Neither does it uni- " verſally prevail, as the lime-ſtone ſtrata, nor " is it like them equally thick; but in ſome " inſtances varies in thickneſs from ſix feet " to ſix hundred. It is likewiſe attended with " other circumſtances, which leave no room " to doubt of its being as much a lava, as that " which flows from Hecla, Veſuvius or Etna."

A ſecond

A second reason, which induced the English naturalist to regard the toad-stone as a real lava of posterior existence to the formation of the calcareous beds, is, that the vertical fissures with which the latter are occasionally intersected, are filled with toad-stone; which necessarily infers the pre-existence of these fissures, and consequently that of the calcareous, strata.

5. The second bed of lime-stone. This is about thirty-three toises thick, of a grey appearance, and contains a number of petrified marine bodies, among which may be distinguished *cames* of a large size, madrepores, &c. The stone is not in all parts of equal hardness. The softer parts, which emit a disagreeable smell on being rubbed with iron, are used for making lime. The harder parts are cut into shape, receive a polish, and answer the same purposes as marble. Some parts of it are penetrated with a siliceous matter in which are several entrochi.

6. Second bed of toad-stone, which is forty feet thick. Mr. Ferber says, " that in " the mine of Hubberdale, this stone deviates " so much from its ordinary hardness that it " has a perfect resemblance to soft clay." But this alteration, which is doubtless observed

ferved in fome pits, is merely local; and the toad-ftone of the fecond bed, as Mr. Whitehurft juftly ftates, is of greater folidity than that of the firft. A circumftance worthy of attention is, that it contains no cavity, and confequently no particles of calcareous fpar.

7. Third bed of lime-ftone; grey, like the fecond, and, according to Mr. Ferber, feventy yards thick. Mr. Whitehurft fays, that it contains fewer petrefactions than the preceding ones, and that it is thirty fathoms thick.

8. Third bed of toad-ftone, refembling the fecond, and twenty-two feet thick. " In the " mine of Hubberdale," fays Mr. Ferber, " this ftone has the confiftence of a tender " and foft clay of a green colour, and is filled " with fmall nodules of black clay, and fe- " veral veins of white calcareous fpar. It is " denominated channel."

9. Fourth bed of lime-ftone. This is grey, like the preceding, but a little whiter. Its thicknefs is yet unknown; feveral parts of it having been dug to the depth of forty fathoms, without difcovering its bottom. It is therefore uncertain whether this fourth calcareous bed be again fucceeded by toad-ftone.

The

The direction of the veins of metal is in general very irregular; the seam is diftinct and well marked; its depth varies, being fometimes feveral feet only, and at others feveral toifes thick.

But what is truly extraordinary and may be regarded as a phenomenon in mineralogy, is, that the veins, which are very rich in the four calcareous beds, always difappear, as they approach the ftrata of toad-ftone, which alternate with the former, fo that it is neceffary to penetrate through the whole mafs of toad-ftone, however thick, in the direction of the feam, without any trace of the ore, until the calcareous bed be reached, where the miners are fure of re-difcovering it. Thus, for example, when a vein is exhaufted in the firft bed, that is, in the firft black lime-ftone, the ore difappears on reaching the toad-ftone, and no veftige of it is found till the bed of toad-ftone has been entirely dug through. " This phenomenon," Mr. Ferber juftly fays, " is, without contradiction, one of the moft " rare and fingular in its kind; and to ac- " count for it is no lefs difficult. Another " fingularity refpecting the beds of toad-ftone " is, that this fubftance fo completely feparates

" the

" the different strata of lime-stone, that an
" inundation of a gallery in the first bed no-
" wise disturbs the labours in the second,
" and that the miners may be dry in a lower
" gallery, whilst all the galleries above it are
" filled with water."

From violent disruptions of the ground, at periods too remote to be traced, the beds are found sunk to a great depth in some parts, while they are much nearer the surface in others. New adventitious and calcareous substances, transported by subsequent convulsions, have filled up many of these chasms, and thus partly concealed the first ruggedness of that wonderful country; but the deep excavations which the miners have made through a great extent of the elevated flat of the Peak, have furnished the means of obtaining an exact knowledge of the topography of Derbyshire, of which I have just here given a slight sketch. More detailed explanations will be found in the work of Mr. Whitehurst, who has given very accurate engravings of the plans, and profiles of the most interesting sections of the mountains.

Impressed with the importance of the subject, I had stopped several times before I reached

reached Buxton, at the foot of some crags where the toad-stone was visible, for the purpose of examining it. With the same view I now asked Dr. Pearson, whether, in his work on the mineral waters of Buxton, he had particularized any bed of toad-stone which we might visit together, assuring him, that any information which he could give me would be so much the more gratifying, as nothing that I had yet seen in that part of Derbyshire bore the least trace of a volcano? I further observed, that a stone in every respect the same as the toad-stone, which he regarded with Whitehurst as a real lava, was found on the high Alps of Champsaur in Dauphiny; that it presented precisely the same varieties of toad-stone, with particles of calcareous spar, with empty cellulæ, and without any spar, often imporous, sometimes hard and compact, at other times tender, tending to decomposition and changing its colour, and that it was sometimes found in the form of small prisms, which led me to think that we might probably meet with it here in the same state.

I mentioned also, that M. De Lamanon, a very estimable naturalist, who fell a victim to his ardour for natural history, in a voyage round

round the world with La Peyrouſe, had written a pamphlet tending to demonſtrate that the ſtone of Champſaur was a product of ſubterraneous fire; and that he for ſome time conſidered himſelf the diſcoverer of an extinct volcano in the Alps; though very able naturaliſts had affirmed that thoſe vaſt mountains exhibited no veſtige of volcanic combuſtion. I added, however, that M. De Lamanon, whoſe opinion I combated, relinquiſhed his error and ſuppreſſed the whole impreſſion of his work, with the reſerve of twelve copies, to each of which he had the honourable firmneſs to annex a printed recantation; that thoſe few were ſent to the moſt zealous of his opponents as an acknowledgment that the ſtones which he had taken for lavas were merely trapps, and that he had the goodneſs to ſend me one among the reſt*.

* See my eſſay on trapp-ſtones, in which I have traced the itinerary from Grenoble to the mountain of Chaillot-le-vieil, in the Alps of Champſaur, with a deſcription of all the varieties of trapp, in every reſpect like thoſe of Derbyſhire, in a much higher country; for the mountain *Peyre-Niere* (Pierre noire) or *Haut-Puy*, which is about one thouſand four hundred toiſes above the level of the ſea, is covered to the top with real toad-ſtones, that is to ſay, trapps.

Excurſion

Excurfion in the Vicinity of Buxton with Doctor Pearfon.—The Stratum of Toad-ftone which he defcribes in his Book on the Mineral Waters.—A fmall Ifle in the River Wye formed entirely of Toad-ftone divided into Prifms.

" Let us fet off then," faid Doctor Pearfon, " I fhall be very happy to fhew you the " bed of toad-ftone that I have defcribed, " and you will tell me what you think of it." We directed our courfe to the hollow which forms the bed of the little river Wye, which, if we may judge by the channel which it has worn, fwells into a torrent with rains. We afcended its banks for nearly a mile towards a corn-mill.

Before reaching the mill, particularly on the right bank, and immediately under the vegetable foil, are fome beds of black fchiftus which vary in thicknefs and exfoliate in fmall pieces on being expofed to the air. This fchiftus is fometimes covered with a flight efflorefcence of martial vitriol; it is the fame which the miners called *fhale* or *fhiver*. This bed of fchiftus, which is in fome parts three, and in others two feet thick, and which conceals itfelf at intervals under the vegetable foil, soil, pursues the same direction to the verge of the mill where it entirely disappears.

Here the nature of the ground suddenly changes; the valley diminishing into a narrow strait formed by two calcareous hills, approaching each other. Between these the mill is erected: the construction of the channel must have suggested this as a very proper situation.

The calcareous rock is of a grey appearance, and its strata incline towards the bed of the river on both sides; but so vigorous is vegetation in this humid region, that, except in a few places, the rocks are completely covered with mosses, lichens, heath, and other creeping plants.

The road leading to the mill runs along a natural causeway formed by the rocks which are entirely bare in this deep hollow. A little above this mill the road is crossed with a bed of toad-stone several feet thick, the black colour of which forms a striking contrast with the grey lime-stone.

This is the bed of toad-stone which Doctor Pearson has drawn as alternating with lime-stone. But on examining it attentively, I observed to this naturalist, that it was difficult

cult to determine whether it was a real bed or a kind of vein; the numerous chafms which muft have formerly exifted in both the hills, from the falling in of the furface, and the vegetable earth with which they have been in general filled up again, fcarcely permit one to afcertain with any degree of certainty the exact and primitive difpofition of the calcareous beds.

On an infpection of the parts where the toad-ftone is uncovered, it appears rather to interfect tranfverfely than to follow the direction of the calcareous ftrata, a fact, which if fufficiently afcertained, would be completely deftructive of the Doctor's hypothefis founded on the ftratification of the calcareous beds in alternate order with toad-ftone.

An attentive obfervation, indeed, of this fmall valley or hollow, formed by the fubfidence of the intermediate fpace through which the Wye now flows, warrants the fuppofition that the chafms, cavities, and fiffures occafioned by the fhock and falling in of fuch enormous maffes, have been again filled up by a fecondary depofition and alluvion, proceeding from a revolution pofterior to that which produced them.

Thefe

These reflexions I submitted to the consideration of Doctor Pearson, stating, at the same time that my conjecture would have still greater probability if we should find the toad-stone lying in a mass above the lime-stone, at the bottom of the valley.

Whilst I was making these observations, I cast my eyes on a small isle of an oblong form, situated in the very center of the place in question. "Let us see," said I, "whether that kind of natural mound, "which has by its resistance, forced the river " to divide into branches, consists of the same " stone as the neighbouring hills."

Doctor Pearson said, that he had not directed his enquiries to that spot. We then repaired to the small isle, which is about a hundred paces long, and from ten to twelve paces broad, but which must have been much more considerable, before it was worn away by the water. It rises only a few feet above the river.

With equal pleasure and astonishment we discovered that it was entirely composed of a blackish brown toad-stone, filled in some parts with particles of calcareous spar, and in others thinly maculated, or without any at all. But what I regarded as most remarkable was,

was, that the first or uppermost stratum of toad-stone, which is about two feet and a half thick, is in several places divided into prisms which form the most exact representation of a small basaltic causeway. It is still farther astonishing, that it affects all the various appearances of the round balls of basaltes, which are often found beside the prisms, or into which the prisms themselves are sometimes changed by the mouldering of their angles. These balls are formed of concentric layers, and exfoliate in the same manner as those of basaltes *.

* " Trapp," says the celebrated Bergmann, " is some-
" times found in the form of triangular prisms, though this
" is a rare case. It sometimes has the appearance of im-
" mense columns, such, for instance, as the *Traſtlemary* at
" the foot of the mountain of *Hunneberg*, opposite to *Brag-*
" *num*, which have detached themselves from the rest of
" the mass. The first time I saw them, they formed an
" angle of eight degrees with a line perpendicular to the
" horizon. For almost all the mountains of Westrogothia
" that have a stratified form, the upper bed consists of
" trapp. It is important to observe, that this bed always
" reposes on a black alluminous slate. Is it possible then
" that this matter should have been in a state of fusion
" without the slightest diminution, even in the point of
" contact, of the blackness of the slate below it, though it is
" evidently alterable by the heat of our common fires? We
" have a still finer trapp, which generally runs in veins,
" and is frequently found in very ancient mountains, in
" which not the faintest marks of subterraneous fire can
" be seen."
Lettres de Bergmann a Troil, page 448, de la traduction
des *Lettres sur l' Iſlande.*

These

These prisms and balls are in a state of commencing decomposition; they are of a brown colour, and sometimes of a yellowish iron grey. Their texture is often intermixed with numerous particles of calcareous spar, the colour of which is frequently stained with the tints produced by the decomposition of the toad-stone. This stone, so divided into prisms and balls, reposes on a bed of friable and gravelly matter, which is in reality nothing else than toad-stone decomposed and reduced to the form of a sandy earth.

It must be acknowledged that nothing can be more volcanic in appearance than this little isle of toad-stone. A vein of this matter, which has considerable resemblance to a current of lava, crosses the calcareous rock which forms the bottom of the mill-road, and then sinks and loses itself in the Wye, so as to lead one to imagine that it has given rise to the isle, which is composed of a substance, which, in the parts where the particles of calcareous spar have been destroyed has the colour and appearance of certain porous lavas, and is further possessed of prismatic and spherical configurations. There is nothing, how-

however, really volcanic, either in this place or its vicinity.

This ferves to fhew the utility of correct local defcriptions to the progrefs of natural hiftory, and the importance of having, in certain circumftances, an opportunity of feeing fubftances in their native place.

The fubftance of toad-ftone is a compofition of filiceous and argillaceous earths, with a fmall quantity of calcareous earth and ron. The proportions of the component parts differ according to the varieties of the toad-ftone. That of Derbyfhire, which is the fubject of our prefent enquiry, has been analyzed by Doctor Withering, who found that in *a hundred parts of this ftone there are fixty-three parts of filiceous earth, fourteen of argillaceous earth, and feven of phlogifticated iron.*

I myfelf, alfo, analyzed a piece of the fame ftone which was broken off from a part that had no calcareous particles; the refults which I obtained were a little different. From a hundred grains of it the produce was as follows:

VOL. II.   x   Siliceous

Siliceous earth — 54 grains.
Argillaceous earth - 19
Aerated calcareous earth 8
Aerated magnefia 4
Iron - - 13
Loft during the procefs 2

Total 100

In making other experiments on ftones of the fame kind, taken from different beds, I always found the fame conftituent principles, but with greater or lefs variations in the refults; fometimes the iron, and at other times the calcareous or argillaceous earth, being in greateft quantity. In a word, and to conclude this already too long and fatiguing difcuffion, the toad-ftone of Derbyfhire, is entirely foreign to volcanos, and is precifely the fame with the Swedifh trapp *.

Some

* If the reader wifh for ftill further information refpecting this ftone, he may confult page 7, 23, 31, 43, and 53, of the work which I have publifhed on trapp-ftones; where he will find that the *argilla martialis indurata* of Cronftedt, the *fchwartzftein* of the Germans, the *toad-ftone, channel, cat-dirt*, and *black clay*, of Derbyfhire, the *whin-ftone* of the Scotch, and the *variolite du drac* of fome Frenchmen, are nothing elfe than trapp in a greater or lefs degree of hardnefs,

Some may perhaps blame me for wishing to generalize too much the name given to a stone which is in the class of compounds, and which itself serves as the basis of several other stones. But I have never pretended to affix the denomination trapp, exclusively of all others, to stones, abounding in the matter of trapp, in those cases where they are diversified by a peculiar character. I have not, for example, ceased to use the terms porphyry, amygdaloides, variolite, &c. though trapp be the basis of all these stones.

I perfectly coincide with the opinion of my illustrious friend, M. de Saussure, that "when " two fossils exhibit any remarkable differ- " ence of character we are not to refrain from " distinguishing them by different names, on " the pretence that there are intermediate " varieties which appear to unite them, by " being equally referrible to either *."

It is with the view of closely adhering to this principle, that, whilst I still preserve the

---

ness, and more or less altered. This stone also forms the basis of the most part of porphyries, &c. &c But whilst I wish to retain the genuine term trapp, I would conjoin with it the different vulgar names which the miners use to distinguish its various modifications.

* Voyage Dans les Alpes, in 4to. Tom. iv. p. 127.

genuine term *trapp*, which must be respected, as it has always been used by the mineralogists of the north, I would apply it by way of preference, and specifically to that stone in every case where it has the hardness, the colour, and the homogeneous appearance which is peculiar to itself, and is void of any very distinguishable extraneous body. But when it contains any particles of calcareous spar, I would call it, with the miners of Derbyshire, *toad-stone*. When the trapp, however pure, has lost its hardness, and its original colour, particularly when it inclines to a greenish colour, and when I at the same time find it in the form of small veins intersecting rocks of another nature, would I never hesitate to call it *cat-dirt*; and thus I would proceed with respect to all the other known modifications as often as they are sufficiently distinct. This is the most simple manner of making ourselves understood, and at the same time respecting the works and the memory of those naturalists who have cleared for us the thorny paths of science.

CHAP-

CHAPTER XVIII.

Caſtleton.—Deſcription of the Cave called The Devil's Arſe.—Mines of Lead and Calamine, Veins of Fluor Spar.—Lead found in Channel or Cat-dirt.

WE rode from Buxton to Caſtleton, a diſtance of twelve miles, on one of the fineſt days of autumn, but along a road as diſagreeable and fatiguing as the worſt of winter.

During our ſtay in this little place, which is agreeably ſituated in the midſt of ſome mountains, we had an opportunity of ſeeing the different workmen in fluor ſpar, and viſited the magnificent cavern called the *Devil's Arſe*, near Caſtleton, and likewiſe ſeveral mines in its vicinity. The reſult of my obſervations is as follows :

DESCRIPTION OF THE CAVE OF CASTLETON, VULGARLY KNOWN BY THE NAME OF THE DEVIL'S ARSE.

This cave, regarded at all times as the principal of the ſeven wonders of Derbyſhire, has

has been celebrated by feveral poets. But as, fince the time of Homer, Virgil, and Ovid, who united extenfive knowledge to fublime talents, few poets have pretended to fcientific correctnefs in their defcription of phyfical facts, I fhall not here repeat any of the verfes, with which the Englifh Mufes may have infpired thofe who have defcribed this grand work of nature.

I feel more fatisfaction in telling my readers, that this cave has been honoured with the vifits of feveral refpectable men of fcience, among the lateft of whom were, Sir Jofeph Banks, Prefident of the Royal Society of London and Dr. Solander, accompanied by Omai, a native of the South Seas, who was received with the moft lively intereft in England, where he remained a confiderable time, and after being loaded with prefents, was generoufly conveyed back to his own country.

This cavern is fituated at the foot of a vaft range of rocks thrown up by nature on the fide of a fteep mountain, upon which ftands an old caftle, built, it is faid, in the time of Edward the black prince.

The principal entrance is 120 Englifh feet in width, and forty in height; it forms a circular

cular arch which opens in a rock of grey, and somewhat sparry, lime-stone, sufficiently hard to admit a fine polish, and containing a number of marine petrifactions, among which the entrochi and some *anonymæ* of a very large species, are the most common. This stone, on being rubbed against a hard body, gives a smell somewhat like that of burnt corn, and some parts of it, which are of a deeper grey and more sparry grain than the rest, emit so strong a smell, that it may very justly be classed among the *lapides suillæ* or stinking stones.

An inhabitant of the place who gains a subsistence by conducting strangers into the interior of the cave, having learnt our arrival, came to wait upon us. He first presented each of us with a printed paper containing the most ridiculous and exaggerated details of the extraordinary things which were to be shown to us, preceded by the following short preamble; " As many persons have com-
" plained of the exorbitant sums demanded
" by those who show this cave, it is proper
" the public should be informed of what ought
" to be given, as those who shew it pay no
" rent to the king. One person ought to pay
" two

" two shillings and sixpence (about three
" French livres); and a party at one time,
" five shillings. These prices, however, are
" not fixed; and the public may give more
" or less as they choose. J. HALL."

J. Hall has adopted in this preamble a very ingenious mode of taxing his customers. But I must do him the justice to acknowledge that he is very active and obliging, anticipates every question, and does not fail to give the most minute details respecting those objects which he conceives deserving of remark. In short, he is perfectly master of his lesson, and recites it with a consequential gravity and sometimes with a tone of enthusiasm, calculated to attract the attention of those who are under his guidance in this darksome cavern.

A party of Englishmen joined us, and we entered the outer porch. It is lighted from without, is forty-two feet high, a hundred and twenty feet wide, and two hundred and forty-six feet long. The light was pretty strong at the entrance of this vast vault, but gradually diminished as we proceeded inwards, or as the fore parts were broken into projections of a greater or smaller bulk. The effect
is

is fo much greater as the fcene is enlivened with two manufactories, the one a rope yard, and the other an inkle ma.. actory entirely within the place.

All is life and motion in this apparent folitude. On the one fide are feen young girls turning their wheels, winding up their threads, and lightening their labours with their fongs, and on the other, men fpinning cords and twifting cables, or forming them into coils. What is ftill more extraordinary, there are two houfes in this fubterraneous apartment ftanding oppofite to each other, entirely feparate from the rock, with roofs, chimnies, doors, windows, and inhabited by feveral families.

It is difficult, without having feen it, to conceive the effect produced by the view of two houfes in a fitu... of this kind. We were foon furrounded with feveral groups of young girls, fome of whom were very handfome.

It appeared that J. Hall here yielded the pre-eminence to the ladies of the place, referving exclufively to himfelf the privilege only of exhibiting to the more profound caverns; all thefe young girls flocked to fhew

us

us the rope and inkle manufactories, and the interior of the two dwelling-houses; after which they directed our admiration to the beauty of the vestibule, the great height of the vault, and the curtains of stalactite which decorate it.

They called our attention more particularly to a stalactite of an extraordinary form at the beginning of the principal arch, a little beyond the farthest house, and at the height of about thirty-five feet. "See," said they, "the fa-"mous *leg of pork*; observe its excellent "shape, and admire this master-piece of na-"ture." But the more we examined this pretended *leg of pork* the more did we find it resemble an object which young girls are not often permitted to examine, and of which they are still more rarely permitted to allow an examination to others. This object was a heart and not a leg; but it was a heart of the same kind as that of M. de Bouflers. This shews the facility with which young folks may be persuaded that they see what they do not see; but it is at the same time a proof of their amiable candour and innocence. Decency, however, demanded that we should preserve a grave and serious countenance.

Testi-

Testifying our grateful sense of their services by a small present, we took leave of them, and proceeded under the auspices of Hall, who, after distributing to each of us a lighted flambeau, opened the door of a subterraneous gallery at the bottom of the grand vestibule, and desired us to follow his steps through the darksome labyrinth of which he willingly held the clue.

The way appeared at fir neither agreeable nor easy. In some places we proceeded in an upright and free posture, whilst in others parts the vaults were so low, that we were obliged to stoop as we advanced, to avoid striking against the protuberances of the rock. This first gallery is a hundred and forty feet long. Here we observed a quantity of sand accumulated into a small oblong eminence. Hall, who was attentive to the minutest circumstances, did not forget to excite our admiration at this sand, which was the production, he said, of a small stream issuing from a subterraneous tank, which we should soon reach. This stream swells after heavy rains, and carrying along with it considerable quantities of sand, often renders the cave inaccessible during its overflow.

Our

Our guide, ſtill advancing and accompanying his obſervations with expreſſive geſtures, entertained us with an account of the rapidity of the current, the height of the water, its quality, and the noiſe which it made; when a ſmall lake, with a ſkiff floating upon it, interrupted our progreſs. This lake, which is not much more than three feet deep, is wholly incloſed in the ſolid rock, and ſtretches under a very low vault of which we could not ſee the farther end. Here it was neceſſary to ſtop.

We ſtood for ſome time on the brink, and the light of our diſmal torches, which emitted a black ſmoke, reflecting our pale images from the bottom of the lake, we almoſt conceived that we ſaw a troop of ſhades ſtarting from an abyſs to preſent themſelves before us. The illuſion was extremely ſtriking.

This piece of water was about forty-eight feet broad; J. Hall gave it the name of the firſt water. He informed us, that we muſt croſs it one by one in the ſmall ſkiff, ſtretching ourſelves at full length, as we had to paſs under the vault which was very low and narrow; he aſſured us, however,

ever, that the paffage was not attended with the leaft danger.

Count Andreani embarking firft, ftretched himfelf flat in the bottom of the little veffel which was furnifhed with fome ftraw. The guide then entered the lake and bending his head almoft to the furface of the water, pufhed forward the skiff with one hand, while he carried his torch in the other.

Five minutes were fufficient to crofs over, and to return for another paffenger. My turn having arrived, I lay flat on my back like the others; but in attempting to move as I paffed through this low and narrow tunnel in order to examine the ftone of which it is compofed, my hat ftruck againft the roof, and was thrown into the water. I was fafely landed on the inner bank, where we filently waited the arrival of fome new companions.

It is impoffible for the adventurer, however cheerful his temper may be, not to trace in this fcene a reprefentation of the paffage of the dead in the fatal bark of Charon. The whole retinue being now landed, Hall, after firft drying himfelf a little and warming his infide with a bumper of rum, which he drank to the health of his followers, called our attention to the fpacious extent of the place which we had now entered. We found ourfelves in a cavern a hundred and twenty feet high, two hundred and twenty feet long, and two hundred and ten broad. It excites real aftonifhment to difcover fuch extenfive natural excavations in the centre of the hardeft rock, and one is loft in conjecturing what has become of the materials which muft have formerly occupied thofe vaft vacuities.

In a paffage at the inner extremity of this vaft cavern, we again met with water, which our guide called the fecond water. But we eafily paffed over on a platform running along the fide of this fmall pond, which is only thirty feet in length.

On iffuing from this paffage we again found ourfelves in a vaft cavern. At the entrance projects a pile of rocks, from the fummit of which the water trickles flowly and depofits a calcareous fediment. This projection has been transformed by the imagination into a houfe, though it has not the fmalleft refemblance to one, and as the water inceffantly drops from it, the genius of rain is fuppofed to have made it his habitation. It is accordingly

ingly diſtinguiſhed by the name of Roger Rain's houſe.

A little beyond this we came to the grand cavern which bears the name of the *Chancel*. The vaults here are very lofty; and in their ſides are different cavities reſembling gothic portals and windows. Large ſtalactites deſcend from the roof upon the prominent parts of the rock, in the manner of drapery or curtains, and produce a very ſtriking effect. The pavement alſo is very ſmooth, being formed of ſolid rock, covered over from time to time with ſome ſtalagmites. The whole has the appearance of a gothic church.

As we advanced our conductor made ſigns to us with his hand, and by expreſſive geſtures, to preſerve ſilence, as if he wiſhed to inſpire us with a reſpectful awe; and he particularly deſired each of us, in a very low voice, not to look behind until he ſhould give notice to do ſo. He then aſſembled his company in a group, and placing himſelf at our head with his face towards us, continued to walk backwards, as if teaching us the military exerciſe, ſtill making ſigns and geſtures in order to attract our whole attention, and inceſſantly requeſting us to keep our eyes fixed on himſelf,

left

left any on sh^{ou}ld be tempted to look behind. Having in this manner reached almoſt the inner extremity of the cavern, he defired us to halt. We then heard fweet and harmonious voices which feem to burſt from the lofty roof, and involuntarily turning round to fee whence the angelic founds proceeded, we obferved in a natural niche at the other end, about forty-eight feet from the bottom, five figures dreſſed in white, immoveable as ſtatues, holding a torch in each hand, and finging in parts a fublime and melodious air to fome verfes from Shakefpear.

It thus appeared that Mr. Hall was playing off his grand machinery for our entertainment; he was delighted even to exultation with the furprife which it produced in us. This unexpected fcene, indeed, made a very lively and agreeable impreſſion on us. It had a melancholy and affecting character, which might be afcribed lefs perhaps to the air and words than to the profound and remote place where they were fung, and where we feemed to be fecluded from the reſt of nature. Thofe of the ancients who felected fimilar places for their initiations, appear to have admirably managed their bufinefs. Their grand myſte-

ries

ries were never celebrated but in subterraneous caverns.

The chantresses disappeared as soon as they had finished their song, and we proceeded in our course through a lengthened gallery. We had been listening to angels, and we had now to make a short visit to the infernal regions. Our master of ceremonies, J. Hall, introduced us into what is called *the Devil's cellar*. Here we saw a great number of names inscribed on the walls. I know not whether those who wrote them have entered into a compact with the evil spirit, and whether out of gratitude he has permitted them to drink all the wine in his vaults; but this much is certain, that the cellar is at present very ill provided. However as there is no entering a cellar without tasting with the butler, especially in England, Mr. Hall pulled out his small bottle, swallowed a glass of rum, and offered each of us a glass after him, but we begged to be excused.

On leaving this gloomy mansion, which is nothing else than a large cavity blackened by the smoke of lamps and torches, we suddenly came to a heap of quartzose sand. Here it was necessary to proceed along a rapid descent a hundred and fifty feet long, and sinking to the depth of forty feet below the level of the entrance. On one side of this sandy path is a deep channel, hollowed by nature in the solid rock, through which a pretty large stream, rising at a distance, gently murmurs along, until it loses itself, with loud noise, amidst some caverns.

Here J. Hall played off upon us one of the little tricks of his vocation. He told us in an emphatic tone, that this subterraneous brook, notwithstanding the total privation of light, produced fish, but of a species which he called black fish. To give us a proof of his assertion, he descended to the water through a narrow passage, and after plunging his hand repeatedly into the stream, held up to our view, at a considerable distance, one of his black fishes. He was about to throw it back into the water to prevent the destruction of the species, which he said was already become scarce, when, upon approaching to take a nearer view of it, I soon found it to be a tadpole which he had carried with him for the purpose of deceiving us, and which was already half dead. He was himself the first to laugh at the cheat, and he candidly confessed it, as soon as he perceived that it was detected.

Proceeding

Proceeding forward, we soon paſſed under *the arcades*, a place ſo denominated becauſe the rock here forms three diſtinct circular arches, very much reſembling thoſe of a bridge.

A little beyond this we heard the noiſe of a diſtant caſcade, and ſaw a pyramidal maſs of ſtalagmite, which is named *the Tower of Lincoln*. Here the cavern was formerly thought to terminate; but, a few years ago, a new gallery was diſcovered, which extends four hundred and ninety-two feet farther. This we traced to its inmoſt extremity, where the little river again appeared to our view, iſſuing from a natural tunnel as perfectly conſtructed as if it had been the work of art, but ſo ſtrait and low, that there was no poſſibility of penetrating into it. At the entrance of this ſort of aqueduct we ſaw ſeveral names engraved in the rock, among which we diſtinguiſhed thoſe of Sir Joſeph Banks and Dr. Solander, and alſo that of Omai, who accompanied them in this ſubterraneous journey.

The entire length of the cavern, from its entrance to the place where theſe inſcriptions are, is at leaſt two thouſand ſeven hundred and forty-two feet.

We performed our vifit, which lafted feveral hours, without the flighteft accident, and returned equally fafe. We made a liberal acknowledgment for the fervices of our guide, who was much more fatigued than we were, as he was inceffantly occupied in pointing out and defcribing the various objects in our courfe. He appeared to be as well fatisfied with us as we were with his zeal and obliging readinefs to ferve us; and though he was a little chagrined at the difcovery of the black fifh, we took leave of each other very friendly.

FLUOR SPARS.

Fluor fpar is an important article of production from the lead mines of Caftleton, in which it is found in greater abundance than any where elfe. The violet is the moft common kind, and ferves as the falband to the white fort. Several other kinds are alfo found there; fuch as fine yellow topaze coloured, violet blue, violet purple, white inclining to rofe colour, water coloured, &c. There are fome pieces, in which feveral of thefe colours are united and produce a very agreeable effect.

Fluor

Fluor fpar would be the moft beautiful of all fubftances, if it were only a little harder. This ftone not only forms a confiderable object of traffic in its rough ftate, between Caftleton and Derby, Winfter, Matlock, Buxton, and other parts in the vicinity, but is alfo worked on the fpot into vafes and other articles of ornament, which are fent to Birmingham, where they are mounted with gilded copper or any other metal.

The largeft pieces of fluor fpar do not much exceed a foot in thicknefs, and are very rarely found of that bulk.

LEAD MINES.

The lead mines of Caftleton are not very rich, and not more than fixty perfons are employed in them; the principal productions of thefe mines being the different kinds of fluor fpar above mentioned.

Several mines have been opened in the very fteep calcareous mountain of *Mann-Zor.*

Oden mine is at a very little diftance from the town, and prefents a very extraordinary mineralogical phenomenon, confifting of a glitter-

glittering galena, which is here called *flikons-fides*. It is usually found in large pieces, forming a double vein. The intermediate space is only a few lines broad, and is filled up with a very white and ponderous gypseous earth, to which the workmen give the name of *keble* or *caulk*.

To break away large pieces of this glittering galena, they make use of a sharp iron wedge, which they drive with a hammer into the thin bed of keble that separates the two veins.

On performing this operation the miners retire with great haste to a distance; and a few minutes after the veins break asunder, with a terrible noise and a general concussion, which must overturn all the props of the roof, if they had not carefully provided against such accidents by strengthening the principal beams with walls formed of the rubbish, and leaving no vacant space. The miners assert that a hollow noise precedes the explosion, and marks the moment when they must consult their own safety by a speedy retreat.

This terrible phenomenon takes place also in the mine of *Lady Wash* near the village of *Pyam*, in the same district of Derbyshire.

Mr.

Mr. Whitehurst has given a very correct description of all the circumstances connected with this phenomenon. Mr. Ferber, who has likewise mentioned it, says, that no reason could be assigned to him for this extraordinary effect; but that he conceives it to arise from an effort of the air, which is strongly compressed, especially in the narrowest parts of the vein, to procure itself a passage.

But to be capable of deciding upon a matter of so much difficulty, it would be necessary to observe with attention all the circumstances that precede and accompany the explosion, to know whether there be any inflammation or smell. It would be proper also to analyze with the minutest exactitude the substance of the gangue, and the keble, which is not yet sufficiently known.

The theory of gas might tend to throw great light upon this phenomenon. It is known that the phosphoric acid is sometimes found in union with lead. The effects of inflammable gas intermixed with phosphorus are likewise well known, and that it kindles with such rapidity by the mere contact of atmospheric air, as to produce the most violent explosions. This branch of science, indeed, is now sufficiently advanced to enable an intelligent obferver, who fhould have an opportunity of tracing all the circumftances upon the fpot, to give a fatisfactory explanation of this aftonifhing phenomenon.

TOAD-STONE CONTAINING LEAD ORE.

Mr. Whitehurft and Mr. Ferber affirm, that in all the mines which have been yet opened, the vein of ore is found exclufively in the limeftone, and difappears fo completely on reaching the bed of toad-ftone, that not the fmalleft veftige of it is difcoverable in the latter; but that on piercing through the toad-ftone, however thick, the vein as certainly makes its reappearance, and this fact they affirm holds good through every feries of ftrata to any depth. This difpofition, however aftonifhing, is in general true, and thence Mr. Whitehurft conceived the opinion that the toad-ftone which thus feparates the calcareous ftrata and interrupts the courfe of the ore muft be the refult of different currents of lava. My thoughts upon this fubject have been already explained, but if there fhould ftill remain any doubt that the toad-ftone is not a product of volcanic

fire,

fire, the fact which I am now going to ftate will be fufficient to remove them.

Doctor Pearfon having fpoken to me at Caftleton of a miner who fold felect fpecimens for the cabinet, we went to pay him a vifit. I purchafed from him a collection of the moft interefting minerals of Derbyfhire, and fome fine fpecimens of fluor fpar, the cryftals of which were in the moft perfect prefervation.

In the courfe of converfation with him, I afked whether it was true, that no vein of ore was ever found in the toad-ftone? he replied, that fuch had uniformly been the fact hitherto, and though long employed in the mining bufinefs, he had never heard that the flighteft trace of lead had been difcovered in that ftone; but that he had juft learned to his coft that the rule was not without exception, if not in refpect to the toad-ftone, at leaft as to the cat-dirt or channel.

On requefting a further explanation, he told me, that he had been ruined by working on his own account, a vein, which at firft had the moft promifing appearance, but which, after opening a deep gallery, at a great expence, was loft in a bed of channel, where,

how-

however, it was again recovered, but in too poor a state to indemnify him.

As the mine was but a little way off, he offered to shew it to us, especially when he perceived that I doubted his account. Providing himself therefore with some mining implements, he desired us to follow him, and we willingly complied.

We directed our steps about a mile to the east of Castleton, along the steep side of the mountain which fronts it, and upon a narrow road about 200 feet above the subjacent plain. The mountain is calcareous, and in some parts exhibits traces of strata; but its general disposition presents a uniform and continuous mass like most calcareous rocks of great elevation. Marine bodies are not very abundant here; I observed, however, a few fragments of entrochi and some terebratulæ. Several lead mines have been opened in it, and it also affords calamine in an ochreous form.

We soon reached the entrance of the gallery which penetrates in an horizontal direction, and opens in the stratified part of the calcareous rock, in a seam of white calcareous spar, which presents a small but very distinct diftinct vein of galena intermixed with fluor fpar.

This indication, which was regarded as very promifing in a mountain which contained feveral other lead mines, determined Elias Pedley and his affociates to commence their operation. But fcarcely had they reached the depth of twelve feet when the lime-ftone terminated, and they had the misfortune to meet with the channel.

As, till then, there had never been any inftance of the moft flender veins of metal being found in this unproductive ftone, they would have immediately difcontinued their labours, had not the fame vein of galena, which they traced through the lime-ftone, continued its courfe in the channel or trapp. This appearance was fo extraordinary and novel, that feduced by it, the miners purfued the ore in the channel to the horizontal depth of ninety feet, in the conftant hope that the vein, which never exceeded an inch in thicknefs, would foon enlarge its dimenfions.

But the farther they proceeded they found the trapp become fo hard, and it required fo much labour and expence to cut through it, that Elias Pedley told us, he was on the point of altogether abandoning the work. This bed of trapp was little more than seven feet thick, but it is very probable that it extends a great way into the mountain, when it is confidered that the gallery had been already carried ninety feet in an horizontal line without difcovering any appearance of alteration.

This bed of channel, or cat-dirt, is really a greenifh trapp, very hard in the interior of the mine, but upon being taken out of the gallery and expofed for fome time to the atmofphere, it becomes friable, its colour changes, and it paffes into an earthy ftate. It is probable that this decompofition arifes from fome invifible particles of pyrites, which become efflorefcent and caufe the fubftance to fall into a detritus.

Here then is a proof that galena has been found in a bed of channel, in which it has been traced in an uninterrupted line of ninety feet, accompanied with a fmall portion of calcareous and fluor fpar. This inftance exhibits a direct and unequivocal exception to the obfervations hitherto made refpecting the mines of Derbyfhire. The exiftence of lead ore in the trapp is a certain proof that it is not the product of fire. I know that thofe mineralogifts

ralogifts who are converfant in the ftudy of lithology, who have examined the trapp upon the fpot, and are fully acquainted with that ftone and all its varieties, have no need of this proof. But the fact appeared to be of fo much importance that I conceived it proper to mention it, to do away every doubt upon the fubject. This confideration, therefore, will form my excufe to thofe who may be difpleafed at the minute and tedious details which I have been obliged to enter into, that I might place the queftion in the cleareft poffible point of view.

CHAP-

CHAPTER XIX.

Derby.—Richard Brown, a Dealer in Curiosities of Natural History.—A Manufacture of Vases, and other Workmanship, in Fluor Spar.

SATISFIED with what we had seen at Castleton, we left that little town, and returned to Buxton; where I put in order the collection I had made of the most remarkable curiosities of Derbyshire.

All our business being finished, we waited upon Doctor Pearson, thanked him for the kind attention he had paid us, and left Buxton next morning for Derby. This journey occupied eight hours, though we had excellent horses and good postillions, but the road was very bad.

Derby is a commercial town. We saw a number of manufactories of different kinds; several porcelain works, and common potteries. We had been informed that a person named Richard Brown, who dealt in natural curiosities, resided here, and that he had in his possession not only the finest productions of

Derbyshire,

Derbyshire, but minerals from different parts of England and Scotland: We visited him. His shop was well replenished with vases of every form and every size, as well as other works in fluor spar of different colours, but much better cut and of a finer polish than those sold at Buxton and Castleton. I purchased a complete collection of his spars cut into small square tablets, in such a manner that they might be placed in drawers, which is the best method of keeping them for study, and the most convenient arrangement for a cabinet.

We were told that Mr. Brown charged very high for his curiosities, but we found that he sold even those which were most interesting and of the finest workmanship at a very reasonable price. He was far from seeking to take advantage of us because we were foreigners; on the contrary, he was moderate in his demands, and treated us with the greatest civility. When he saw that I was fond of lithology, and that I named some stones with respect to the nature of which he was doubtful, he testified much happiness at seeing us, and begged that we would stop with him and drink to the friends of the science of nature.

nature. He inftantly ordered glaffes and feveral kinds of wine to be brought; but as we had juft been drinking after dinner, we declined this invitation, of the kindnefs of which however we were very fenfible, for Mr. Brown preffed us with the greateft cordiality.

While we were difputing this point of politenefs, a dog, which I had purchafed in the highlands of Scotland, fuddenly left me in the ftreet: he differed from the common fhepherd dog. The Scottifh dog has more ingenuity and manages a flock of fheep better than the ordinary kind. It is alfo excellent for keeping off the fox. I tried, but in vain, to recover this animal: my dog was loft or rather ftolen.

Next day we went to fee another vender of articles of natural hiftory, who was himfelf a worker in fluor fpar and marble. He refided at one of the extremities of the town, by the fide of a fmall river, which flowed at a fhort diftance from his houfe.

He was a very intelligent young man. I never any other where faw vafes of fuch perfect forms, fuch exquifite lightnefs, and fuch fine materials; but his prices were higher and his manners lefs accommodating than
thofe

thofe of Mr. Brown; wifhing, however, to take fomething from him, I purchafed a vafe which charmed me by the beauty of the colours of the fpar, its elegant form, and the delicate finifh of the workmanfhip. This dealer had alfo fome of the minerals of Derbyfhire for fale, but in his collection of them I found nothing interefting.

CHAPTER XX.

Departure from Derby.—Arrival at Birmingham.—Its numerous Manufactures.—Doctor Withering.—Benjamin Watt.—Doctor Priestly—His House, Library, and his chemical Elaboratory.

WE left Derby at noon, but as the roads were all very bad in this quarter of the country, we had some difficulty in arriving on the same day at Birmingham. At nine in the evening we entered an inn in this town, after having crossed some black arrid heaths, and passed through a savage and dreary region.

We had letters of recommendation to Doctor Withering, the translator of the Sciagraphia of Bergman, and a lover of botanical and chemical studies: We waited on him next day. He inhabits a fine house, furnished with taste and elegance. We had tea with him in company with some amiable and beautiful ladies, and to complete our good fortune, we were here introduced to Mr. Watt, a man of singular merit, one of the most skilful mechanists of England, and who possesses great knowledge in chymiftry and natural hiftory.

The extenfive commerce and manufactures of Birmingham render it one of the moft interefting towns in England: Here the traveller may have a comprehenfive view of a moft active and varied induftry exercifed in the different arts of utility, of pleafure, and of luxury.

I know that fome travellers who have not fufficiently reflected on the importance and advantage of manufactures in a country, fuch as England, have difapproved of extenfive works of the kind eftablifhed in this town. I know that even Englifhmen who have taken but a hafty and inconfiderate view of thefe magnificent eftablifhments, have obferved that it was difficult for the eye to be long pleafed in the midft of fo many frivolous arts, and where the labours of a hundred men are confined to the making of a tobacco box*. But befides that this ftatement is exaggerated, thefe travellers have overlooked the vaft works where fteam engines are made, thefe aftonifhing machines, the perfecting of

* See Gilpin's Picturefque Tour.

which does so much honour to the talents and knowledge of Mr. Watt; the manufactories constantly employed in making sheet copper for sheathing ships bottoms; those of plate-tin and plate-iron, which render France tributary to England, and that varied and extensive hard-ware manufacture which employs to so much advantage more than thirty thousand hands, and compels all Europe, and a part of the new world, to supply themselves with these articles here, where every thing is made in greater perfection, with more economy and greater abundance, than in any other country.

I must observe here, what cannot be repeated too often to Frenchmen, that it is the abundance of coal which gives this advantage, and produces, in the midst of a barren desert, a town with forty thousand inhabitants, who live in plenty, and enjoy all the comforts of civilized life.

The various manufactures in which this useful mineral is employed have covered a sterile and sombre heath with groves of lillies and roses, and converted a savage wilderness into fertile and delicious gardens. The works established by Messrs. Boulton and Watt, in which more than a thousand hands are employed,

ployed, have contributed greatly to promote this change.

The population of Birmingham encreafed fo much during the American war, that at leaft three hundred new houfes were, during that period, added annually to the town. At the conclufion of the peace, this increafe was doubled. The gentleman who made me acquainted with thefe facts, and who poffeffed much information, one day fhewed me a new ftreet of confiderable length, in which the conftruction of the houfes was juft commenced upon an uniform plan, and the building was carried on with fo much rapidity that there was little doubt but the whole would be finifhed in lefs than two months.

I experienced much pleafure in vifiting Mr. Watt, whofe extenfive knowledge in chymiftry and the arts, rendered his converfation very interefting. His moral qualities, and the engaging manner in which he expreffed his thoughts, daily encreafed my refpect for him. He has a number of fine children, who are all diftinguifhed by their information and their talents.

I dined one day with this agreeable family, when Doctor Prieftly, who is a relation of

Mr. Watt, was prefent; I had the pleafure of forming an acquaintance with this celebrated man, to whom experimental philofophy owes fo many obligations. I afterwards vifited him in company with Mr. Withering. Doctor Prieftly does not refide in Birmingham, but at the diftance of about a mile and a half from the town, in a charming houfe, with a fine meadow on the one fide, and a delightful garden on the other. There was an air of the moft perfect neatnefs in every thing connected with this houfe, both without and within it. I know not how to give a better idea of it than by comparing it to thofe fnug houfes fo often to be met with in Holland, particularly on the road from Harlem to Leyden, and from Leyden to the Hague.

Doctor Prieftly received me with the greateft kindnefs. He prefented me to his wife and his daughter, who were diftinguifhed by vavacity, intelligence, and gentlenefs of manners. The young lady fpoke to me of one of her brothers, who was then finifhing his education at Geneva, and to whom fhe feemed very much attached.

The building in which Doctor Prieftly made his chemical and philofophical experiments was

was detached from his houfe to avoid the danger of fire. It confifted of feveral apartments on a ground floor. Upon entering it we were ftruck with a fimple and ingenious apparatus for making experiments on inflammable gas extracted from iron and water reduced to vapour. The tube, which was thick and long, was made of red copper and caft in one piece to avoid joinings. The part expofed to the fire was thicker than the reft. Into this tube he introduced cuttings or filings of iron, and inftead of dropping in the water, he preferred making it enter in vapour. The furnace deftined for this operation was fupplied with coak made of coal, which is the beft of all combuftibles for the intenfity and equality of its heat.

By thefe means he obtained a confiderable quantity of inflammable gas of great lightnefs and without any fmell. He obferved to me, that by increafing the apparatus and ufing iron or copper tubes of a larger calibre, aeroftatic balloons might be filled with far lefs trouble and expence than by vitriolic acid. Doctor Prieftly allowed me to take a drawing of this new apparatus for the purpofe of communicating it to the French chymists who are engaged in the same pursuit.

The composition which Doctor Priestly used to prevent the gas from escaping, either in this or other experiments, appeared to me so excellent that I begged of him to tell me how he made it. He informed me, that after a multitude of trials, he had found nothing answer the purpose so well as the paste of almonds, such as it is when the oil is extracted. This moistened with a little water, in which glue had been dissolved, made an excellent lute. He observed, however, that the glue might be dispensed with.

Doctor Priestly did not regard the experiments made relative to the decomposition of water as satisfactory. He could not admit the fact to be demonstrated so long as the gas was only obtained through the medium of iron, a metal which is itself susceptible of inflammability; but he waited with impatience for the result of the experiments of the French chymists, particularly those of Lavoisier, who had invented, and caused to be constructed, an extensive apparatus for the same object.

" The decomposition of water," said this indefatigable philosopher, addressing himself

to

to me, " is of so much importance in natural
" philosophy, and would occupy so distin-
" guished a place among the phenomena of
" the universe, that far from admitting the
" fact upon slight evidence, and as it were
" from enthusiasm, it were rather to be wish-
" ed that all objections that may be made, and
" which will still long continue to be made
" against this theory, were completely refuted:
" In the conflict of opinions, truth may at
" last be obtained. But I have still so many
" doubts upon this subject, and I have so many
" experiments to make, both *pro* and *con*,
" that I can as yet regard the question as
" only started *."

Doctor Priestly has embellished his soli-
tude with a philosophical cabinet, which contains all the instruments necessary for his experiments, and a library rendered valuable by
a choice of excellent works. The learned

---

* Mr. Benjamin Watt, who has published some excellent papers upon the theory of fire, was of the same
opinion with Dr. Priestly. " The theory of the decom-
" position of water is seducing," said he to me, " as it
" would be convenient for explaining the different pheno-
" mena of nature; but the more I reflect on this delicate
" subject, and upon all that has hitherto been done and
" written relative to it, the more I find it involved in diffi-
" culties."

poffeffor employs himfelf in a variety of ftudies: Hiftory, moral philofophy, and religion, have all in their turn engaged his pen. An active, intelligent mind, and a natural avidity for knowledge, gave him a paffion for experimental philofophy; but the fenfibility and gentlenefs of his difpofition have fometimes directed his attention to pious and philanthropic ftudies, which do honour to the goodnefs of his heart, fince they always have for their object the happinefs of mankind. Befides his fituation as a preacher, renders it often neceffary for him to fpeak in public *.

Next day I had the pleafure of meeting Doctor Prieftly at Mr. Watt's, where we partook of an agreeable repaft, in company with feveral amiable and intelligent men.

---

* I fhall not here detail the perfecution which this worthy man experienced fince the period in which I faw him. His chymical elaboratory, his cabinet of natural philofophy, his library, his charming houfe, were all deftroyed by barbarous fanatics. The government has endeavoured to repair this lofs by proportional indemnities, which amounted to fifteen hundred louis. But wifhing, as a philofopher, to fly from intrigue and to feek repofe, and defirous of avoiding fimilar dangers, he has retired to the United States of America. Let us hope, that in this afylum, he may profecute his ftudies with his ufual zeal, and that he will be able to repair in part the lofs of his valuable manufcripts.

Mr.

Mr. Watt is a man of great conceptions. Nature has endowed him with a very vigorous mind, and to his other excellent qualities he joins the mildeſt and moſt prepoſſeſſing manners which intereſt even at firſt fight.

Mr. Watt ſhewed us a corn-mill, which he had conſtructed, and which was ſet in motion by a ſteam engine. The application of this principle to the mechaniſm of a mill is a happy idea, which may be very advantageouſly applied in a country which has few ſtreams, and is rich in coal. This firſt attempt will lead to others, and the principle will ſoon be applied to a number of uſeful purpoſes *.

Mr.

---

* Since this period ſimilar mills have been ſuccesſfully erected at Nantes, and ſome at Paris, where ſome ſteam engines are uſed for ſtamping coins. Steam engines were firſt eſtabliſhed in France, by the brothers Periers, who joined much activity to a great deal of knowledge : But theſe excellent machines cannot reach the perfection they have obtained in England, until our government ſhall ſeriouſly turn its attention to the opening of coal mines. Thoſe who know the exhauſted ſtate of our foreſts are convinced that the moment will ſoon arrive when we ſhall be obliged to work them from neceſſity. Thoſe who are acquainted with the neglected ſituation of our coal mines, tremble, leſt it ſhould hereafter happen that we ſhall want both wood and coal at the ſame time. There is ſome reaſon for anxiety on this ſubject, when we conſider that at Paris a weigh of bad coal coſts ſix times more than the beſt did ſome years ago. But if the legiſlature were to turn to

the

Mr. Watt is so familiar with great inventions, possess so much knowledge in the higher branches of mechanics, and has brought the means of execution to so much perfection, that he may justly be ranked among the men, who have chiefly contributed to create the present high prosperity of the useful arts and commerce in England. He is a native of Scotland : A country which has long been accustomed to supply England with men who honour it the most in every science and profession.

We passed several days at Birmingham, where we may be said to have resided in the midst of the arts and industry. The society of enlightened men and amiable women added new charms to our situation. Our minds were informed and delighted; our heads were filled with facts, and our hearts with gratitude. Such were the pleasures we experienced in this town. We left it with regret.

the consideration of this subject, as well as that of canals, with the earnestness they deserve, it would be found that our resources of this kind are as inexhaustible as those of another kind, which we have already exhibited to the astonishment of all Europe.

CHAP-

CHAPTER XXI.

Departure from Birmingham.—Coventry.—Warwick.—Oxford.—Saint Albans.—Barnet.—London.—Return to France.

As we were preparing to leave Birmingham, Mr. Watt requested to know whether we could take under our care one of his sons, who was to go to Paris, and thence to Geneva. We answered, that it gave us a great deal of pleasure to be able to afford him a seat in our carriage, in which there was sufficient room for his accommodation, and that we should pay every possible attention to his son, who was a very engaging young man. Count Andreani and myself were extremely pleased to have an opportunity of justifying the confidence which Mr. Watt reposed in us, and of proving to him how happy we were to be able to give him that small mark of esteem and attachment.

On leaving Birmingham we were delighted to see the country on every side studded with gentlemens seats possessing a simple but elegant

gant appearance, which was greatly heightened by the effect of the rofy colour of the bricks upon the white ground of the ftone work. Every thing here was fo much more ftriking, as thefe elegant habitations were almoft new. But fcarcely had we loft fight of them, and paffed through fome words, when we entered upon an extenfive tract of wild and barren heaths.

Between Birmingham and Coventry we had a view of an ancient manfion belonging to Lord Aylesford. It is not very agreeably fituated, but it was eafy to fee that the proprietor had employed the affiftance of tafte and art in embellifhing it.

Coventry is a pretty neat little town. The fpire of the church is feen a great way off. The foil here confifts of broken flints intermixed with reddifh earth.

From Coventry to Warwick we paffed over a flat country, in fome places woody, and in others naked, and with a foil like the preceding.

We ftopped at Warwick in order to vifit the church, which is a very fine ftructure in the gothic ftile. The chapel where the chiefs of the houfe of Warwick have been interred,

and

and where is feen the tomb of the earl of Leicefter, is charged with fculptures and gothic ornaments of the moft finifhed neatnefs. Having vifited the other curious monuments of the place, which are defcribed at length in feveral productions, we proceeded on our way to Stratford, celebrated as the birthplace of the immortal Shakefpeare. We croffed the river Avon by a bridge of fourteen arches, erected at the expence of one Hugh Clifton, who was a mayor of London, and a native of this town.

We next reached Oxford, where we vifited the moft remarkable monuments of fcience and art. But all thefe are already fo generally known, that it would be fuperfluous to defcribe them. I fhould have been happy to have met here with Mr. Thompfon, a very excellent naturalift, with whom I had formed an acquaintance at London, whence he had gone to fettle at Oxford. But he was unfortunately abfent from home. It would have been not only very agreeable, but alfo very ufeful to us to have feen him, as he could have introduced us to the learned men of the place, to whom, from a reliance upon his prefence, we had not provided ourfelves with any recommendation.

From

From Oxford we proceeded to London through Saint Albans and Barnet.

Our ſtay at London was not long. Having taken leave of our learned friends, who had kindly gratified us with the numerous objects of inſtruction and entertainment, which that city affords, we ſet out for Paris, where we arrived five days after. Count Andreani prepared for his return to Milan, young Watt took the road to Geneva, and I remained at Paris.

FINIS.

.

www.ingramcontent.com/pod-product-compliance
Lightning Source LLC
Chambersburg PA
CBHW020229240426

43672CB00006B/468